THE UNTOLD STORY ABOUT HOW UNIONS TOOK OVER ILLINOIS GOVERNMENT

Who is actually running Illinois government? It's not the administration. It's not the department heads. It's the public employee unions.
—Chicago Tribune, November 25, 2019

DR. NORMAN JONES

authorHOUSE

AuthorHouse™
1663 Liberty Drive
Bloomington, IN 47403
www.authorhouse.com
Phone: 833-262-8899

Published by AuthorHouse 08/22/2022

ISBN: 978-1-6655-6854-8 (sc)
ISBN: 978-1-6655-6852-4 (hc)
ISBN: 978-1-6655-6853-1 (e)

Library of Congress Control Number: 2022915169

Print information available on the last page.

DEDICATION

This book is dedicated to members of unions in Illinois, past and present, whose civil rights were infringed on by an employer and who were not legally represented by their unions. The US Supreme Court has held that unions must provide "fair representation" for union members. That is not happening in Illinois. Ignoring this federal statute is a plot by unions so they don't have to spend their money on what could be expensive lawsuits. This scheme allows unions to pay union employees high salaries and contribute to campaign funds of lawmakers who favor union causes.

The book is also dedicated to retired FBI agent Steve O'Reilly, who helped inspire me to write the book. It could not have been written without his help. Once I sent him evidence of unions violating federal law, he was very patient and helpful in clarifying what the unions were doing that was illegal. He said, "This case belongs in federal court," and explained that "Illinois is not adhering to the supremacy doctrine afforded the Supreme Court."

My writing is also dedicated to my family. Sadly, my wife Patricia passed away before the book could be published, but she is remembered as a beautiful, loving wife. I could not have married better. The book is also dedicated to my three daughters and their families. They are Denise Luksetich, her husband, Rick, and their two boys, Eric and Adam. Diane Stratton, her husband, Eric, and their three children. They are Jack and his wife, Lindsey; Danielle and her husband, Caleb Taylor, and Jamie Stratton. Deborah and her husband, Bob Struck, and their twins, Lyla and Logan.

CONTENTS

CHAPTER 1

It All Started in Peoria

The *Chicago Tribune* made a stunning comment in an editorial in November 25, 2019. It stated, "Who actually runs Illinois state government? It's not the administration. It's not the department heads. It's the public employee unions." I was not surprised at such a comment because many teachers (including me) had problems with the teachers union that I was a member of during my thirty-two-year career in education. The union was the Illinois Federation of Teachers-American Federation of Teachers-AFL-CIO. I was employed by the Palatine School District 211 and a member of the local 211 union.

As of writing this report, the *Tribune* has failed to inform the public what Illinois unions have done to position themselves so that they can run the government. Obviously, being able to run the government is a tremendous advantage to unions because the state legislature adopts laws that affect union power and finances. This book is titled *The Untold Story about How Unions Took Over Illinois Government* because I reveal how almost all of the moves unions have made in the last forty-some years have helped enable them to finally control the Illinois government. It's worth mentioning that no investigative reports have appeared in the *Tribune,* and no editorials have mentioned the strategic moves that the unions made to take over the state's government. Exactly how unions took over the government remains a secret, but secrecy is the enemy of democracy. And so the untold story about the unions taking over must be told.

1

I believe an event that happened in Peoria, Illinois, in 1983 was the catalyst that motivated unions to establish power and remain solvent. Terry Knapp, a high school teacher in the Peoria system, filed a First Amendment lawsuit against the district. He had been retaliated against in various ways after he spoke out about the school board's policies. The federal court in Chicago awarded Knapp over $500,000 in damages. The Peoria school board appealed to the US Supreme Court, and the amount was later adjusted to about $350,000 when the case was remanded to the Illinois federal court for review. Knapp was represented by IFT-AFT-AFL-CIO lawyers, and the union had to pay his enormous legal fees. Those fees came out of union dues, the financial life blood of unions. It is very likely that when this union determined that several costly cases like this could be devastating to union funds, it decided to never again fund lawsuits. In fact, the union made Knapp use his winnings from the lawsuit to pay the union lawyers. When asked by a reporter to comment on his victory, Knapp told reporters that regarding his financial gain, "The lawyers took most of it."

Union employees are paid using the dues that unions collect. Somehow, word got passed around to Illinois union heads that funding expensive lawsuits must be curtailed. The problem with this decision is that unions are required, by law, to "provide fair representation to members," when their rights are infringed by unscrupulous employers. In fact, two US Supreme Court cases (*Vaca v. Sipes* and *Hines v. Anchor Motor Freight*) held that unions have a statutory duty to use their funds to defend members and cannot act in an arbitrary, a discriminatory, or in bad faith. One federal judge ruled that unions cannot plead poverty when they claim not to have funds to defend a member. Supposedly, the fair representation doctrine protects individuals against arbitrary union conduct. These federal statutes were intentionally overlooked when Terry Knapp had to use his winnings to pay the union lawyers. It is pure speculation whether Knapp would have had to pay them out of his own pocket had the case been lost.

I firmly believe that shortly after the IFT-AFT-AFL-CIO made the decision not to provide funding to protect member rights, the Illinois Education Association, an affiliate of the National Education

Association, and other unions decided to do the same. The IFT-AFT and the IEA-NEA are the two largest educational unions in Illinois. The Chicago Teachers Union (CTU) is an arm of the IFT-AFT, like the other educational unions.

After years of following union activity, I now believe that *all* unions in Illinois, public or private, have discovered that they can save a great deal of money by disregarding federal law and even meritorious cases brought by dues-paying members. Clues to this plot exist. Tonya Exum, an employee of the Ford Motor Company near Chicago and a member of the United Auto Workers (UAW), published an op-ed in the *Tribune* titled, "Why Am I Paying Union Dues When My Union Won't Protect Me from Sexual Harassment?" (photo 1). The UAW is a private-sector union.

Why am I paying union dues when the union won't protect me from sexual harassment?

BY TONYA EXUM

What happens when a female union member in Chicago reports sexual harassment in the workplace? If she's a member of the United Auto Workers, nothing.

Well, that's not completely accurate.

She'll get rebuked for tattling on a union brother. She'll be bullied into tolerating the disgusting as normal. She'll be belittled for being sickened by graphic images and demeaning comments. She'll get brainwashed into believing that an attack isn't harassment if it only happened once. And she'll realize her cries to her union for protection are meaningless because of the inherent conflict of interest that exists when a union tries to represent both the victim and her attacker.

That's my experience as an autoworker, UAW member and victim of sexual harassment.

I've worked at Ford's stamping plant in Chicago Heights for five years. I began working as a production team member on the assembly side of the plant and I was literally harassed by lewd comments from Day One. Smacks on the bottom were a common occurrence. I was frequently groped by my male colleagues to the point that it prevented me from doing my job.

Such harassment was not an isolated experience; it was pervasive behavior afflicting every corner of the plant.

I called the harassment hotline several times, which yielded nothing. While media outlets have recently exposed Ford's role in perpetuating a dangerous workplace culture, and rightly so, the UAW also played an important role by

standing between me and the accountability I sought. I often complained to the UAW, which was supposed to represent my interests, only to hear crickets in return. I am now a plaintiff with about 30 other employees in a lawsuit against Ford Motor

Co. and these allegations are included in the lawsuit.

In my experience, the worst perpetrator of sexual harassment was actually a union representative. And it wasn't just sexual harassment: As I allege in the lawsuit, I've been

run off the road by this man, he's slashed my tires, and he's even come to my house to bother me. (I had to have my teenage son chase him away.)

Little did I know the UAW would protect him at all costs. The union has a conflict of

interest. Because the perpetrator was also a union member, it has to represent me and represent my predator. I even had one UAW rep tell me: "You know, it's not sexual harassment if they only do it one time. You shouldn't report it."

Then I asked myself: Why am I paying union dues when the UAW won't even protect me from sexual harassment? And if Ford isn't going to take appropriate action against my harassers, shouldn't I be able to get help from my union? Shouldn't my union stand up for me against Ford?

The union's rhetoric was a slap in the face. But it only reaffirmed my desire to seek out other women who experienced similar types of harassment. And find them I did. I joined a lawsuit with other Chicago women to not only hold Ford accountable, but also to fight back against a union refusing to do its job. On Thursday, I'm scheduled to testify before a state legislative task force to describe our fight against harassment.

While we lost our battles in the workplace, dozens of us are now taking the fight to court, where we hope to finally hold company officials accountable for their wrongdoings. A victory will not only bring justice to Chicago, but it may even inspire a new generation of women to fight back against their tormentors.

But my other message to them is this: Don't expect your union to have your back. #MeToo.

Tonya Exum is a production team member at Ford's Chicago Stamping Plant.

CENTER FOR UNION FACTS

Tonya Exum says the harassment started almost immediately after she started working at the plant.

Exum reported that she was rebuked when she asked her union to protect her from sexual harassment. Exum stated,

> I was literally harassed by lewd comments, smacks on the bottom were a common occurrence. I was

frequently groped by my male colleagues to the point that it prevented me from doing my job ... I often complained to the UAW, which was supposed to represent my interest, only to hear crickets in return. I am now a plaintiff with about 30 other employees in a law suit against Ford Motor Co. and these allegations are included in the law suit.

There was no mention of Exum filing suit against the UAW, but it seems plausible that the UAW should be held accountable to protect her interests. She said, "Don't expect your union to have your back."

I included Exum's op-ed because it's a good example of the conduct of Illinois unions that don't want to file lawsuits to defend members when their civil rights are infringed by unscrupulous employers. As mentioned earlier, such arbitrary behaviors likely started with the Knapp case. Ignoring employee complaints is intentional and has the aim of saving unions money. This is a major ploy to keep union coffers stable, so they can buy off politicians with campaign donations. These donations, popular in Illinois, lead to buying off state legislators, who are then influential in favoring the legislations that keep unions strong.

The IEA-NEA took similar steps to avoid paying heavy attorney fees. It announced to members on its website that "if you need legal help you can get that help at rates below usual attorney fees." Still, this policy meant that union members would have to pay heavy legal fees to defend themselves, despite the fact federal statutes require unions to use their funds to defend their members. One IEA-NEA member was harassed, transferred, and had his salary cut by his principal because he would not change a grade for a student for whom the principal wanted a favor. If the music teacher had changed the student's grade from a C to a B, she would have had a B average and would have qualified for a lower insurance rate on the family automobile under state standards. The union would not support the harassed teacher, even though federal law required it. Union heads at the school were aware that if the teacher filed a lawsuit, it could endanger the union coffer. Snubbed by the IEA-NEA, the teacher now works in management at a Menards in central Illinois.

The problem with unions not using dues to defend the civil rights of its members is that such a policy wantonly violates federal statutes. As mentioned, there are two US Supreme Court decisions that held that "unions must back their constituents," and, "cannot arbitrarily ignore meritorious cases."

The Illinois Policy Institute is a nonpartisan research organization. It believes that "civil and personal liberties must be protected and preserved" (*A Guide to Illinois Government Unions*). The institute does its best to keep citizens informed about unions' activities. In the guide, some interesting comments and facts about union finances were published. Author Paul Kersey, director of labor policy at the institute, made an interesting comment: "Illinois goes to great lengths to cater to union officials, to the point where contracts are hidden from the public until it's too late to change them." This means bills are passed that cater to union whims, keeping them wealthy. How such power was obtained by unions is a big part of the story being pieced together herein. As Kersey has pointed out, this information has been kept in the dark for too long. Kersey astutely stated that unions have grown incredibly powerful and, "how those unions have grown so powerful is not well understood."

The purpose of this book is to have the advent of union power in Illinois totally understood, exposed, and changed for the better by legal action. It is important to remember the sequence of events that show what the unions did to gain their power in Illinois. Recall Terry Knapp in Peoria, Tonya Exum of the UAW, and the music teacher who was harassed out of his job by his principal.

Perhaps even a better example that lends itself to Mr. Kersey's idea that unscrupulous state lawmakers help boost union power is a case that took place in the Chicago Public Schools (CPS). Three pregnant teachers were harassed by a principal who wanted them back at work despite the usual leave policy. The teachers reported the harassment to the CTU, but since such a complaint could lead to a costly lawsuit that would have to be paid out of union funds, the union ignored the complaint. When the teachers reported the case to the US Department of Justice, that office quickly stepped in and settled the case. But the point is that it was the duty of the CTU to protect the rights of the teachers.

Illinois has four powerful unions ignoring federal laws in order to assist unions in their power grab. The four unions are the IFT, the IEA, the UAW, and the CTU.

It is not a stretch to assume that the plot by unions to keep their coffers wealthy and stable so they can continue to pay off influential state legislators continues to this day. Just take a look at the salary structure of some unions, which the Illinois Policy Institute printed in their guide to Illinois unions. First, glance at pages lifted from the Illinois Policy Institute report on union finances in 2011. This is twenty-eight years after the Knapp case, and it shows what many believe are outrageous salaries for union employees. And keep in mind that Knapp had to pay his legal fees despite federal rulings that unions must provide fair representation to members. (See photo 2.)

Illinois Federation of Teachers

2011 spending

Category	Total expenditures	Pct.
Representation	$9,920,935	58.0
Politics and lobbying	$1,377,647	8.1
Contributions, gifts and grants	$22,013	0.1
Overhead	$2,117,747	12.4
Administration	$3,662,245	21.4
Total	$17,100,587	

Notice in this spending chart for the IFT that the cost of administration was $3,662,245. This amount included the salaries of about forty union employees. The top salary of $189,920 was that of the union president, Dan Montgomery. Below him salaries ran down to $127,764 for various jobs within the union hierarchy. Such titles as "legislative" and "field staff" are listed along with "communications" staff. It would be interesting to find out just what these jobs entail.

Illinois Education Association

2011 spending

Category	Total expenditures	Pct.
Representation	$8,626,086	25.3
Political/Lobbying	**$1,631,742**	4.8
Contributions/Gifts/Grants	$153,377	0.4
Overhead	$15,653,294	45.9
Administration	$8,066,807	23.6
TOTAL	$34,131,306	

The spending chart for IEA administration purposes (photo 3) amounts to $8,066,807 and shows the union president, Kenneth Swanson, drawing a salary of $181,593. Nearly a hundred IEA employees made between $151,507 and $126,182, and they included a variety of titles.

American Federation of State, County and Municipal Employees (AFSCME) District Council 31

2011 spending

Category	Total expenditures	Pct.
Representation	$7,292,006	46.7
Politics and lobbying	**$1,093,637**	7.0
Contributions, gifts and grants	$248,238	1.6
Overhead	$4,634,976	29.7
Administration	$2,341,872	15.0
Total	$15,610,729	

The chart for the District Council 31 (Illinois government workers; photo 4) shows its executive director Henry Bayer making $140,779. Other salaries range downward to $110,400 for highly compensated officers and staff. This union does not represent teachers. It represents general government workers such as clerical, administration, and human services workers.

The salaries of union employees are shown here to give credence to the idea that union leaders as far back as the Knapp case in Peoria agreed two things were of the utmost importance to unions in Illinois. Those two things are for unions to pay union employees generous salaries and have plenty of money to contribute to politicians who can influence legislation that keeps unions powerful.

There are literally hundreds of unions in Illinois whose leaders understand the goals developed since the Knapp case. To be able to implement these goals has been a successful plot by union leadership. Don't forget, Mr. Kersey once remarked, "How unions have been grown so powerful is not well understood." This book, this untold story about unions gaining power and taking over Illinois government, can be illuminated by going back and looking at one category in the charts presented about union spending. That category titled "Representation."

In studying in further detail, the charts shown for the spending habits of the IFT, IEA, and AFSCME as representation, it can be seen that large sums of money were doled out for what might look like the unions' duty to follow federal statutes and protect worker rights.

Recall again that Mr. Kersey believes that the advent of union power in Illinois is not well understood. I believe one of the things that needs to be better understood is just what representation really means. What does it cover? This knowledge seems important since it is known that the filing of lawsuits to protect members' rights was pretty much done away with after the Knapp case.

Consider these facts when trying to better understand union finances. The IFT claimed it spent $3,662,245 on administration and $9,920,935 on representation. The IEA spent $8,006,807 on administration and $8,626,086 on representation, while AFSCME spent $2,341,872 on administration and $7,292,006 on representation. Interestingly, finances for the CTU are not mentioned in this report. Administrative payouts were listed for each employee, but where the money was actually spent and for what is not spelled out in the category of representation. I became suspicious. I made some inquires and searched the internet to find lawsuits filed by the CTU, but I came up empty. I could only surmise that the union's plans not to file lawsuits to save money was working for it. It was becoming clear that what happened in Peoria in 1983 to keep unions strong was having its effect decades later.

CHAPTER 2

"We Cater to Unions. You'll See"

The motivation for me to fill in the gaps and make this untold story a fully told story came to me almost by accident. As mentioned previously, I was employed by Palatine High School District #211. I had moved there in 1967 from southern Indiana. The district was not unionized until the mid-seventies. This was the time that the IFT and the IEA began to infiltrate school districts and became rather powerful. And the now powerful CTU was flexing its muscle.

In a strange twist of fate, I became embroiled in a disagreement with the school district administration when I noticed a glaring error in a contract between the union and the district. In that agreement, salary lanes for teachers were established for those based on each year of experience and degrees held. The top lane for the most experienced teachers would receive a $3,600 raise. The next lane, where I was placed, would receive a $2,900 raise. However, the third lane would receive a $3,600.00, the same as the top lane. So I and about forty other teachers in the second salary lane were being cheated out of $700. The error could be easily recognized by a middle-school child.

I called board member Anna Countryman and explained the error. She said, "Norm, that's not right." She said she would bring it up at the next board meeting, before the contract could be ratified. I attended the board meeting and was shocked when she did not bring up the issue for debate. The contract was ratified. And although I didn't know it at the time, that is what motivated me to tell this story, this untold story about how unions in Illinois fail their members

I was a member of the IFT-AFT local #211, and I asked them to check out the error in the salary agreement. I was given short shrift, and the contract was not questioned.

In April 1984, I was told I was being transferred to another school in the district, which would mean a longer drive for me. I would be forced to teach physical education and generally humiliated. But the shocking thing the union did not address was this: I was a full-time counselor at the school and had seventeen years of experience with perfect evaluations. The district had granted me a sabbatical in 1976 to obtain a doctorate in counseling and educational psychology from the University of Mississippi. I earned a 4.0 GPA and wrote a dissertation about how counselors can be more accountable in secondary schools. The dissertation is on file at the University of Michigan.

I realized it was likely I was being retaliated against for speaking out about the error in the salary agreement. I again contacted the union and told leaders that I thought my First Amendment right to speak out was being infringed. Union heads ignored me again, so I filed a First Amendment lawsuit against district #211 in the federal court in Chicago. Months passed, but finally, federal judge James Alesia handed down an order and memorandum that held my case to be meritorious. He noted that since my evaluations declined about the time I was speaking out, I was being harassed, and the case should proceed to court. Of course, I again asked the union for help. It was at this point the union granted me a session with a union attorney. I met with IFT lawyer Mildred Haggerty in Chicago and several officers of the Local #211. At the advice of my lawyer, I had kept a good notebook detailing what the district did to harass me, but they need not be mentioned here. I had the decision of a federal judge and was confident it was the duty of the union to take over my suit and use its funds and lawyers to defend my First Amendment right to speak out about public concerns. What else were unions for? Certainly, the salary agreements between teachers and school districts were of public concern.

During the session with Ms. Haggerty, I showed her a copy of the order and memorandum handed down by Judge Alesia. She alarmingly said that "This union cannot afford to file an expensive lawsuit on your behalf." I was shocked, as were my colleagues in attendance at the conference.

To make a very long story short, my case against my school district was settled out of court, and damages were obtained stemming from the lawsuit.

Once the case was settled, the fact that my union could get away with not providing me legal and financial assistance lingered in my mind. I asked my lawyer what I could do about it. He suggested contacting a little-known board in Illinois, the Illinois Educational Labor Relations Board (IELRB). This board is chartered to settle disputes in the educational arena.

I called this board to file a complaint against the IFT for not backing me in my lawsuit against my district. A spokesman for the board, Ralph Locke, told me, "You can file a complaint, but we cater to unions. You'll see." I immediately thought, *How can a state board cater to anyone?* Right then I smelled a rat. Of course, as it has turned out, I was becoming a victim of decisions made in Peoria in 1983. Unions had made such great progress in protecting their interests that they had infiltrated a state board with the power to rule on cases that could have effects on union finances and power.

I thought it best to file the complaint because I told myself, "I am going to pursue this because it might be important to find out just how a state board can cater to unions." I thought it was important to find out the words used by the IELRB to dismiss my case. I could then report it to the proper authorities and hopefully stop the unions from making moves to keep themselves wealthy.

On July 1, 1992, the IELRB delivered its decision to me. It held that the union did not violate the Illinois Educational Labor Relations Act by allegedly failing to provide me with legal and financial representation. With that statement, I knew that the all-encompassing US Supreme Court decisions about unions having a duty to represent were quickly being shuttled to the background. The unions had, since 1983 in Peoria, somehow cleverly implemented laws that made it so unions did not have to spend their money to defend members. Remember, I was not questioning state law. I was questioning the state of Illinois not abiding by federal statutes. The concocted language used by the IELRB to dismiss my case stated that unless a union could be found guilty of "intentional misconduct," a charging party could not win such a case. One federal judge stated that the intentional misconduct standard meant that a union would have to confess to be found guilty of an unfair labor practice.

It was obvious how the unions had influenced legislation and enacted language to get around applying to federal standards. For example, it was mentioned that I had failed to serve the union with a "certificate of service." It was stated in the decision that "Whenever a document is filed with the Board, it shall be accompanied by a certificate of service. A certificate of service shall consist of a written statement, signed by the party effecting service, detailing the name of the party served and the date and manner of service." This was news to me; I was never informed about such a certificate. I now realized that union members were being forced to jump through many hoops if they were to gain representation by their unions.

The IELRB ruling stated, "Because Jones failed to serve his exceptions and attach a certificate of service," the case was dismissed. It was pathetic that the IELRB stated, "This Board is governed by the Illinois Educational Labor Relations Act, not by the myriad of federal cases cited by Jones." Such a statement made it clear to me that federal law governing unions is cast aside in Illinois.

More skullduggery by the IELRB could be seen when it was stated in the decision that union attorneys gave my case a full review. The fact was that union attorneys never talked to any of my sixty-five witnesses or even read the depositions in my case. Yet, this inaction to protect a union member was not considered intentional misconduct.

I noticed at the very end of the IELRB ruling against me it stated that any appeal of the order must be taken directly to the state appellate court. I now realize that unions helped to make this decision in the hope charging parties would not take the case to federal court, where the standards are much higher and more in favor of charging parties.

After going around and around with the union, trying to get them to take over my case, I decided it would be important to find out what would happen with the case in the Illinois Appellate Court. My lawyer filed that appeal, and we received a judgment on May 5, 1995. As expected, the appeals court dismissed the case despite the ruling of federal judge Alesia that the case was meritorious. It became obvious that even the state's appellate courts favored unions. The court even showed favoritism to the union when it mentioned that "Should the union decide to fund the case the union would deplete its somewhat limited resources." Even more, it was beyond disgusting when the Illinois Appellate Court ruled that a labor organization, when asked to fund a lawsuit for a union member, "has no duty to provide such funding." This ruling was a direct rebuke of US Supreme Court's decisions on fair representation. What was even more disturbing about this Supreme Court ruling is that it was handed down over a quarter of a century ago, and absolutely nothing had been done to make unions abide by the law of the land. Only in Illinois! It seemed obvious that the state court was, just as the IELRB, catering to unions.

In 1995, I had to put a stop to using family funds to defend myself. I had two daughters in college, and I told myself I could not justify continuing my effort to expose the crooked unions and the crooked state government. I could only try to follow what unions were doing by clipping news reports or occasionally browsing the internet for information.

CHAPTER 3

Brotherly Love?

Three years after the questionable appeals court ruling, I thought I caught a break and might be able to make another effort to expose what the unions were doing. My brother, Wendell Jones, a former mayor of Palatine, became a state senator. This came about when his friend and colleague Peter Fitzgerald beat Carol Mosley Braun in a race for the US Senate. Peter had been an Illinois state senator, so this left a vacancy, and my brother was appointed to finish out Peter's term.

Of course, I now thought I had a person in state government who might help launch an investigation into union activity I knew had negative effects on union members and on how state government functioned. My brother and I had many conversations about it. I showed him the evidence I had accumulated. By then, I was in possession of the memorandum from federal judge James Alesia, the refusal of the IFT to support my First Amendment case against district #211, the dismissal of my case by the IELRB, and a similar dismissal by the Illinois Appellate Court.

After reviewing my evidence, my brother agreed. "Something must be done about unions, about them not properly representing their members." He decided he would have a better chance to make inroads with the IELRB rather than through the Illinois Appellate Court. He wrote a letter Victor Blackwell, executive director of the IELRB. He received a response from Keith Snyder, an assistant to Mr. Blackwell. I considered that letter prima facie evidence regarding union corruption. The letter in its entirety follows:

May 23, 2003

The Honorable Wendell Jones E. Jones
105C State Capitol
Springfield, IL 62706

Dear Senator Jones,

This letter is a follow-up to the phone conversation we had last evening. There are many different kinds of unfair labor practice charges that in a typical year, the Board will consider over 400 cases. There are nine different types of charges that can be filed against management and six that can be filed against unions. As I understand your concern, it deals with one particular charge: unfair labor practice charges filed against unions for failure to represent their members properly. I'll try to describe for you some of the issues surrounding the union's involving a union's duty of fair representation to its members.

The standard:

The most significant issue that led to the results that were highlighted in the information you provided is the standard, set forth in State law, that employees must meet in order to find a union guilty of an unfair labor practice charge. Section 14 (b)(1) of the Illinois Educational Labor Relations Act states that unions commit an unfair labor practice "only by intentional misconduct in representing employees." The Appellate Court has interpreted "intentional misconduct" to mean behavior that is deliberate and severely hostile, fraudulent or deceitful."

This standard was not in the law when it was originally enacted in 1984.The original standard was conduct that was arbitrary, discriminatory or in bad faith. Labor unions successfully amended the Act in the mid-1990s to add the higher standard. School management groups did not oppose the change since it had no effect on them, so unions had virtually a free hand to craft the standard they prefer the high "intentional misconduct" standard makes it very difficult for employees to prevail against the union in these cases. In fact, in the history of the Board, unions have lost only two of these cases. To successfully prove such a charge, an employee needs meticulous records and virtually a "smoking gun" for evidence to show that the union was deliberately and severely hostile, fraudulent, or deceitful in its inaction. Even if Board members are sympathetic to the issues raised in a particular case, we are required to follow the language of our Act as set forth by the General Assembly and the interpretation of our Act as set forth by the courts. If the evidence does not rise to the standard, we are not free to rewrite the standard.

Timeliness issues:

As was noted in your brother's letter to you, many of these cases were dismissed as being untimely. Again, this issue is another one in which our hands are tied. Our Act says, "no order shall be issued upon an unfair practice occuring more than 6 months before the filing of the charge alleging the unfair labor practice." (Section 15) As with the standard above, the timeliness issue has been dealt with in the courts. They have held that the timeframe is a "jurisdiction" issue, meaning that the law prohibits us from enforcing any unfair labor practice charge, regardless of the severity, that occurs more than 6 months prior to the filing of charge. Our Board has interpreted the language to mean that the clock starts running, not when the conduct occurred, but at the time the employee became aware of the conduct or should have been aware of the conduct. If a charge is not filed within that window, the law and the courts have told us we have no choice but to dismiss the case.

In addition to the 6 month window for filing a charge, there are internal board deadlines for case processing. These deadlines are set forth in our agency rules. Any complaint, whether it is an employee, a union or school management, who misses a deadline can have its case dismissed. The internal deadlines are enforced in the interests of fairness, efficiency and orderliness. The Board does grant exceptions to these deadlines if the circumstances are extenuating and if

The other party will not be harmed by the exceptions.

Procedural issues:

Some of the cases you highlighted were won by the unions on procedural grounds. These grounds would include things like: (1) a complainant failing to provide his or her legal arguments of documents to the other side. (2) a complainant failing to appeal his or her case to the next step, or (3) a complainant failing to cooperate with the Board's investigation of the case. As with internal deadlines, case processing procedures are in place to ensure each party and each charge is handled in a fair, efficient and orderly manner. Failure to follow procedures can lead to dismissal of the charge.

Conclusion:

Your brother is correct that unions rarely lose duty of fair representation cases. The reason for that track record is not corruption on the Illinois Educational Labor Relations Board, however. The primary reason is the high standard that must be met by employees. Timeliness issues and procedural issues play a part as well, but the standard is the real culprit. If you have any further questions or need more information, please do not hesitate to contact me.

Sincerely,
Keith Snyder

P.S. Interestingly enough, when Margaret Blackshere, the head of the Illinois AFL-CIO, testified in the House in favor of elimination of our agency, one of the reasons she gave was that the Board was no longer a Labor Board, but had become, in her words, a "Management Board."

I regard this letter to my brother as the one document that convinced me I had uncovered a plot by people in positions to cater to unions. Mr. Snyder's words compelled me to further investigate union activity in Illinois. Remember when I called the IELRB to file a charge against the IFT? I was told, "We cater to unions. You'll see." Mr. Snyder even agreed that unions had a duty of fair representation, but he gave himself away when he stated, "The standard employees must meet is set forth in state law." That is a misrepresentation of the truth as it is set forth in federal law. In the federal law, the standard is that unions cannot act in an arbitrary, a discriminatory, or bad faith way. However, Mr. Snyder actually changed that to a higher standard when he stated that a union could only be found guilty of an unfair labor practice when it could be shown it acts, "only by intentional misconduct." In chapter 5, where I write about involving the FBI to tell my story, that agency points out that states cannot change or modify US Supreme Court decisions.

In showing how labor unions have increased their power since 1984, Mr. Snyder confessed how the unions changed the federal law: "Labor unions successfully amended the Act in the mid-1990s to add the higher standard." Alarmingly, he noted that "Unions had virtually a free hand to craft the standard they preferred." Does anyone reading this wonder how unions could obtain such authority to craft laws that affect them? The only way unions could have acquired such a free hand was by being able to influence many state legislators since they are the ones who enact the laws. Such influence is paid for with union money, and that is a big reason unions don't want to defend members in expensive lawsuits.

Notice that Mr. Snyder stated, "The high intentional misconduct standard makes it very difficult for employees to prevail against the unions." Actually, by ignoring federal law, states make it impossible. This is what unions want and have cleverly achieved since the mid-1990s. In addition, Mr. Snyder even mentioned that union members must have kept meticulous records and virtually have a "smoking gun" to prove the rigged law of intentional misconduct. He cleverly stated the courts set forth the controlling law. But he suspiciously ignored using the lower standard set forth by the US Supreme Court. He cited the many hoops union members must jump through, which unions successfully installed so they didn't have to spend their money defending members. Things such as meeting time lines to file a case or failing to meet many procedural issues are two of the more obvious deterrents union members have stacked against them. After all the illegal moves the unions and this board made to cater to unions, it was disheartening and beyond disgusting to read that Mr. Snyder reported that this labor act was designed so, "Each party is ensured the case is handled in a fair manner." It is known that the IELRB dismisses all fair representation cases, and that is how this state-chartered board caters to unions to keep money in their coffers. It is sickening that I informed many state and, as will be seen, federal officials of these undeniable facts, yet the silent insurrection continues to this day.

Since I had collected documents that showed the IELRB and the

Illinois Appellate Court were probably in cahoots and manipulating federal laws to help make unions stronger in Illinois, I asked my brother to launch an investigation in to these antics. Even though he had the authority as a state senator to launch such an investigation, he refused. Just before he denied my request, my wife and I watched as my brother sat in the first row of the Senate and voted on some bills. After that session, we met in his office, where I met some of his fellow politicians. After that meeting, we went to dinner. Much to my surprise, my brother told me, "Stop talking about your problems with the union."

"I am going to do what is necessary to make unions back their members according to the law," I responded. With that remark, my brother pounded his fist on the table and stalked out of the restaurant. I never saw him again! Evidently he felt my continuing to fight the unions might put him in a bad light regarding being reelected. I guess he felt my effort to expose the unions might cost him votes.

Unbeknown to me, my wife wrote to my brother and asked him to reconsider and launch an investigation into the activities of the IELRB and the Illinois Appellate Court. She explained to him that it was important to me to expose the illegal actions of these entities. My brother refused to change his mind.

CHAPTER 4

"This Case Is Too Old. Nothing Can Be Done"

After being rebuffed by the IELRB, the Illinois Appellate Court, and my brother, I gave considerable thought to what to do next to expose the unions and the crooked politicians who were—and still are—helping to keep them strong in Illinois. I decided to start with the politicians in my area who were supposedly elected to represent me. At that time, I remembered attending my brother's swearing-in ceremony. He raised his right hand and gave his oath: "I swear to uphold the laws of this state and this nation." I wrote to my state senator, Pam Althoff, and state representative, Jack Franks, and told them about the illegal actions the IELRB and the Illinois Appellate Court were taking. In shocking responses, each of these state officials ignored their oaths and helped to perpetuate the union tyranny going on in Illinois. Senator Althoff wrote and said, "This case is too old. Nothing can be done." She evidently believed, as many members of the General Assembly in Illinois do, that if corruption can get old enough, it is given permission to continue without the threat of investigation. Even more alarming, Jack Franks told me on the phone, "File your own lawsuit. When you become a pauper, then the state can help you."

I asked him, "Where does it say in the constitution that we have to pay for our rights?" Both politicians gave me short shrift in my effort to expose the union caper.

I contacted State Representative Barbara Wheeler about what had now become union tyranny in Illinois. She joined her colleague Pam Althoff in believing, "This case is too old. Nothing can be done." What was really discouraging was that at the beginning of Mrs. Wheeler's tenure in the General Assembly, she posted a comment on her website that said, "What is needed in Springfield is courage and bravery." It was profound, but she took it down. For what reason is known only to her.

I contacted State Representative Susan Bassi, from Palatine, who shared an office in Palatine with my brother. I never heard from her. Silence is just another way Illinois politicians ignore their oaths, "to uphold the laws of this state and this nation," and, therefore, help to perpetuate union power.

It was about this time that my brother's friend, State Representative Bernard Pedersen, came to my house. He listened to me and reviewed the documents I had at the time. He asked me to come to Springfield and testify before the House Labor Committee. He asked me to tell them what I had uncovered about the IELRB, the Illinois Appellate Court, and people who seemed to be involved in furthering union interests. The experience was quite an eye-opener for me. It was given before about fifty members of the Illinois House of Representatives. Mr. Pedersen told me he thought laws should be changed in Illinois that would give teachers a level playing field. He said that in his view, "You are speaking for the teachers in Illinois." Of course, he meant that teachers were being denied fair representation by their unions. I know he had the IFT and the IEA in mind. He said he would sponsor a bill to bring Illinois law in line with federal law requiring unions to provide fair representation for their members.

During my testimony, I saw three representatives talking on cell phones. Others were reading newspapers, and still others were talking in small groups. The inattention to my report was disgusting. It got so bad that Mr. Pedersen stopped my presentation and told the group, "Stop acting like you are kindergartners and pay attention." I got a better understanding of what these legislators thought of the civil rights of teachers and the rights of union members in Illinois. I was observing an "I don't care" attitude, and it was very discouraging.

What was worse than not being listened to was the fact that a woman from the IFT-AFT sat right beside me and lobbied to defeat Mr. Pedersen's bill. I immediately wondered, *Why would a teachers' union not want to have to abide by federal laws that would protect the civil rights of teachers? Why would a union representing teachers want to do anything to hurt teachers? Of course,* I then thought, *this is part of the union's plot to save money.*

Mr. Pedersen did sponsor a bill, but, of course, it was quickly tabled. There is an overwhelming need in the General Assembly for a law that automatically ensures that US Supreme Court decisions become law in Illinois. To adopt such a mechanism would seem more democratic, but those sleuths who have somehow slithered into Springfield to protect the interests of the unions seem to multiply rapidly and increase the unions' power. I agreed with the *Chicago Tribune* columnist John Kass when he wrote, "Supporting the Constitution is a radical concept in this combine state."

I knew Mr. Pedersen's bill would go nowhere. My brother had told me the speaker of the house, Michael Madigan, controlled everything that happened in the General Assembly. I am certain he was instrumental in having Mr. Pedersen's bill tabled because doing so protected the interests of unions. As this is written, Michael Madigan has been indicted for public corruption in other matters.

After providing testimony in front of the House Labor Committee, I became interested in finding out just how widespread union favoritism was in the General Assembly. I was able to obtain a booklet that listed the emails of state legislators. I sent out 114 email messages to some state senators and some state representatives. I urged them to investigate the antics of the IELRB, the Illinois Appellate Court, and the unsavory moves being made by some of the state's largest unions. A few of the politicians sent a reply along the lines of, "Thank you for this information." And a couple called me, but no one took action.

I was, however, taken aback when I received an unsolicited Whistleblower Information Intake Form from the office of Lisa Madigan, who was the Illinois attorney general at the time. I knew she was the daughter of Speaker of the House Michael Madigan. Evidently my 114 emails prompted one of the legislators to contact her, and she responded by sending me the Whistleblower Information Intake Form. I thought it best to include as much evidence as I could about how the IELRB, the Illinois Appellate Court, and unions were flaunting federal law to keep unions powerful. Perhaps the most important question the intake form asked was, "What specific law or regulation was violated, if you know?" I was pleased to enter, "The specific laws being violated are two US Supreme Court decisions, and they are: *Vaca vs Sipes,* 386 U.S. 171 (1967), and *Hines vs. Anchor Motor Freight,* 424 U.S. 554 (1976).

I wish I had been informed of other laws being violated, but I did not have that information until a few years after filing this form. A good labor lawyer I contacted assured me that two federal statutes were being violated. They were, conspiracy against rights and deprivation of rights under color of law. I wish I had been able to inform Lisa Madigan of how these statutes were being ignored.

The form asked very good questions, and I became excited that perhaps my efforts to expose the unions and the corrupted IELRB and the Illinois Appellate Court were paying off for me and the people of Illinois. One question was, "Describe your complaint in detail, including dates, locations and the names of people involved." Another told me to "List all people, besides yourself, who have knowledge about your complaint. Include each person's name, home and work addresses and telephone numbers." Other questions asked if I had documentation and if I had filed a complaint with any court or government agency, and if so, the status of that filing.

It took several hours to fill out and file eleven pages of evidence, documentation, names, addresses, and so on. And I was quite excited to do so. I ended my report to the attorney general saying, "Thank you for sending me the Whistleblower Information Intake Form. I sincerely hope that my report will help clean up Illinois and help restore the reputation of a state that is currently in sad disarray and to the point businesses shy away from coming to Illinois."

While I anxiously awaited a response, I looked up the duties of the office of Illinois attorney general. On Lisa Madigan's office website, it stated that her responsibility was, "To litigate to ensure state and federal laws are followed and respected," and that, "The Attorney General is committed to defending the rights of all the people of Illinois."

I was extremely disappointed and discouraged that it looked like my efforts to expose the crooked unions was going to continue because of the response I received from the attorney general.

OFFICE OF THE ATTORNEY GENERAL
STATE OF ILLINOIS

Lisa Madigan
ATTORNEY GENERAL

October 6, 2010

Norman H. Jones
759 Silk Oak Lane
Crystal Lake, IL 60014

Re: Illinois Educational Labor Relations Board

Dear Mr. Jones:

This letter acknowledges receipt of the Whistleblower Information Intake Form dated September 23, 2010 you submitted and the attached documents. We have reviewed your complaint regarding the above matter and the facts, as we understand them, do not presently warrant further action by our Office.

Under Illinois law, we cannot provide legal advice or represent you as your personal lawyer. Consequently, if you wish to pursue this matter, we suggest you consider discussing it with a private attorney.

This letter is not intended to render any opinion regarding the legal merits of any claim you may or may not have.

Sincerely,

THE OFFICE OF THE ILLINOIS ATTORNEY GENERAL
OF THE STATE OF ILLINOIS

She stated that the facts I sent her, "do not presently warrant further action from our office." Remember, I had given her two US Supreme Court decisions that certainly showed the IELRB and the Illinois

Appellate Court were in direct rebuke of federal law. Better stated, these agencies were in cahoots. I wondered how the chief legal officer in the state could ignore the IELRB deliberately modifying these controlling laws. Furthermore, how could the Illinois Appellate Court get away with ruling that "Unions have no obligation to provide funding to protect the civil rights of members"? I was now even more certain that I had uncovered the unions' plot to save money by not using dues revenue to file lawsuits on behalf of members. It was clear to me that Attorney General Madigan was aiding and abetting this plot to further the causes of Illinois unions.

A few years later I saw Lisa Madigan interviewed on Chicago TV. She was asked point-blank why she wasn't doing more to fight corruption. She responded quickly, "My hands are tied." She did not elaborate, but it can be assumed that state laws, rules, and regulations implemented during her father's reign in office allowed the office of the attorney general to ignore corruption. Alarmingly, former attorney general Roland Burris stated on the same news program, "I never worried about corruption."

Incidentally, I somehow came across an article titled, "Illinois Federation of Teachers/Chicago Teachers Union." The article gave facts about union activity in Chicago and Illinois. Note that the IFT represents 90,000 (in 2006) teachers, and so on throughout Illinois. Interestingly, the names of Democrats from then-governor Rod Blagojevich's administration were listed as career patrons of the IFT and the CTU. From January 1, 1993, through June 30, 2006, the IFT and CTU contributed $6,261,000 to candidates for Illinois statewide constitutional and legislative offices. Ninety-three percent of these contributions were contributed to Democrats. In my mind, these contributions were a big part of the money unions acquired that helped to buy off politicians who favored their agendas. (See photo 6.)

> I found statistics on the internet that showed the IFT represents about 90,000 teachers throughout Illinois. At one point, the IFT and the CTU contributed $6,261,000 to politicians running for offices in state

government, and 93 percent of those were Democrats. In my view, this money was a big part of the union build-up of funds that helped to buy off politicians who favored their agendas.

Armed with the questionable decision of Lisa Madigan, I decided to keep probing the antics of the unions, the IELRB, and the Illinois Appellate Court. I was pleased when Senator Dan Duffy of Barrington agreed to meet with me in his office and discuss why I was now rather certain that the IELRB and other state entities were doing many illegal things, making questionable decisions, and generally maneuvering to advance union power in Illinois. We met for about an hour. It was interesting to me when he said, "I've often wondered about this board and unions." I made my pitch about how the IELRB dismisses every fair representation case that comes before it. I made it clear that these dismissals helped to fuel the plot to control state government because the dismissals allowed unions to avoid filing expensive lawsuits to protect the civil rights of their members. I showed him how the money saved helped unions build their coffers, which allowed them to fulfill two of their priorities: to contribute to campaign funds of politicians who favor unions and to pay high salaries to union employees.

I showed Senator Duffy the letter from Mrs. Madigan that told me that the evidence I sent her, "does not presently warrant further action." I requested that he launch an investigation. Senator Duffy agreed to write to the Office of Executive Inspector General (OEIG) for the agencies of the Illinois governor. Senator Duffy sent me a copy of the letter from Recardo Meza, inspector general at that time.

Notice that the letter (photo 7) stated I had filed complaints about the IELRB ignoring federal law regarding the statutory duty of unions to represent their members. Note also that Mr. Meza does not mention the IELRB by name. He mentions that his office, "declined to investigate because the alleged misconduct occurred more than one year from the date of Dr. Jones' complaint and Section 20-20(1) of the State Officials and Employees Ethics Act prohibits us from initiating an investigation more than one year after the most recent act of the alleged violation."

Dr. Norman Jones

He should know that this type of corruption is going on every day, and the state should not be allowed to enact laws that prohibit investigations into alleged wrongdoings.

OFFICE OF EXECUTIVE INSPECTOR GENERAL
FOR THE AGENCIES OF THE ILLINOIS GOVERNOR

PAT QUINN
GOVERNOR

32 WEST RANDOLPH STREET, SUITE 1900
CHICAGO, ILLINOIS 60601
(312) 814-5600

RICARDO MEZA
ACTING EXECUTIVE INSPECTOR GENERAL

November 1, 2010

Dan Duffy
State Senator, 26th District
330 E. Main St., Ste. 301
Barrington, IL 60010

Re: Complaints to the OEIG made by Dr. Norman Jones

Dear Senator Duffy:

I am writing to follow-up on your letter of September 27, 2010 concerning Dr. Norman Jones. You informed us that Dr. Jones received a letter from this Office, which was sent prior to my appointment, which stated that we declined to investigate a matter because "State laws regulating labor relations between public employers and employees take precedence over federal labor laws."

We have reviewed our files and discovered that Dr. Jones has in fact filed two complaints with our Office in the past year. In the first matter, OEIG Complaint # 09-00566, Dr. Jones withdrew his complaint after being contacted by an investigator from our Office. In the second matter, OEIG Complaint # 09-01025, we declined to investigate because the alleged misconduct occurred more than one year from the date of Dr. Jones' complaint and Section 20-20(1) of the State Officials and Employees Ethics Act prohibits us from initiating an investigation more than one year after the most recent act of the alleged violation.

Unfortunately, we have been unable to find any correspondence in our files indicating that we informed Dr. Jones that we were declining to investigate because State law trumped federal law, which by the way is not true. Federal law trumps state law either if state law is in direct conflict with federal law or if federal law has occupied the field.

In any event, thank you again for contacting our office. I am enclosing a copy of our two most recent OEIG newsletters for your review. If you have any further questions or wish to further discuss this matter, please do not hesitate to contact me at (312) 814-8268.

Sincerely,

Ricardo Meza
Acting Executive Inspector General

Mr. Meza also mentions that "Unfortunately, we have been unable to find any correspondence in our files indicating that we informed Dr. Jones that we were declining to investigate because State law trumped federal law, which by the way is not true. Federal law trumps state law either if state law is in direct conflict with federal law or if federal law has occupied the field." Evidently Mr. Meza's office didn't keep very good records because, as can be seen below in a letter from Deputy Inspector General of Investigations Janet Doyle, she states, "State laws regulating labor relations between public employers and employees take precedence over federal labor laws."

People in state agencies who are bent on helping unions grow and prosper have become experts in formulating language that prohibits investigation of unions. In the cases of Mr. Meza and Ms. Doyle, it can even be seen that Ms. Doyle believes state laws take precedence over federal laws, and Mr. Meza disagrees with that position. Still, with what they told me, the OEIG found a way not to investigate the unruly unions, the IELRB, and the Illinois Appellate Court.

Note in Ms. Doyle's letter (photos 8 and 9) that she mentioned the OEIG was created to investigate misconduct in the agencies, boards, and commissions responsible to the governor. However, she used the illegal and much contrived state law language that a union member must prove "intentional misconduct" on the part of the union to prevail in an unfair labor charge. Interestingly, Ms. Doyle pointed out that a one-year timeline to file a case stands unless there is, "reasonable cause to believe that fraudulent concealment has occurred."

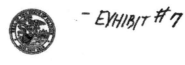

OFFICE OF EXECUTIVE INSPECTOR GENERAL
FOR THE AGENCIES OF THE ILLINOIS GOVERNOR

ROD R. BLAGOJEVICH
GOVERNOR

32 WEST RANDOLPH STREET, SUITE 1900
CHICAGO, ILLINOIS 60601

JAMES WRIGHT
EXECUTIVE INSPECTOR GENERAL

July 5, 2005

Dr. Norman Jones
759 Silk Oak Lane
Crystal Lake, IL 60014

Re: Complaint Number 05-00593

Dear Dr. Jones:

We have received and reviewed your letter containing allegations against the Chicago Teachers Union and the Illinois Educational Labor Relations Board ("IELRB"), which was forwarded to us by Scott Turow, Chair of the Executive Ethics Commission. The Office of Executive Inspector General ("OEIG") was created to investigate misconduct in the agencies, boards and commissions responsible to the Governor. Initially, you understand from our correspondence on your prior complaint (No. 03-00131) that the Chicago Teachers Union is not an agency within the jurisdiction of the Governor; accordingly, our office has no jurisdiction to investigate complaints against the union.

With respect to your claims against the IELRB, while your letter alleges "unethical behavior of top Illinois officials" and "intentional misconduct," an examination of your claims reveals that your true complaint is over the propriety of a State statute, not a State official. Your complaint appears to be that the Illinois Educational Labor Relations Act favors unions over employees, in that it states that a union commits an unfair labor practice "only by intentional misconduct in representing employees." You state that the IELRB should be required to follow the federal standard, under which it is easier for an employee to show that he was denied fair union representation.

The federal National Labor Relations Act ("NLRA") governs labor relations in the private sector; however, states and political subdivisions of states are not employers governed by the NLRA. 29 U.S.C.S. 152(2). Thus, State laws regulating labor relations between public employers and employees take precedence over federal labor laws, and while decisions of the National Labor Relations Board and federal courts are persuasive authority, they are not binding

34

on Illinois labor relations boards. *East Richland Education Association v. Illinois Educational Labor Relations Board*, 173 Ill. App. 3d 878, 902 (4th Dist. 1988).

The Illinois Educational Labor Relations Act ("IELRA") governs labor relations for Illinois public school teachers. 115 ILCS 5/2(a)-(b). The IELRB recognizes a duty of fair representation under the IELRA. See *Paxton-Buckley-Loda Education Ass'n v. Illinois Educational Labor Relations Board*, 304 Ill. App. 3d 343, 348 (4th Dist. 1999). However, as you are aware, in order for a union to breach its duty of fair representation to one of its members, the IELRA requires that the union engage in "intentional misconduct." 115 ILCS 5/14(b)(1). In order to demonstrate "intentional misconduct," an employee must show "substantial evidence of fraud, deceitful action or dishonest conduct." *Paxton-Buckley-Loda*, 304 Ill. App. 3d at 349.

We understand that you disagree with this standard and believe it is wrong; however, only the Illinois legislature can change Illinois law. Your letter indicates that you have taken appropriate steps by bringing this matter to the attention of several Illinois legislators, including your brother, and that you have testified before a labor committee in Springfield in an effort to effect a change in the law.

We note that the letter from Keith Snyder, which is attached to your letter to Mr. Turow, is dated May 23, 2003. Under the Ethics Act, the OEIG may not initiate an investigation "more than one year after the most recent act of the alleged violation . . . unless there is reasonable cause to believe that fraudulent concealment has occurred." 430 ILCS 20-20(1). In addition to not showing any violation of rule, regulation or statute, none of the documents you have provided show any fraudulent concealment that would extend the limitations period set forth by law. Additionally, it is OEIG policy not to investigate matters where there is a more appropriate administrative or judicial process available. In this case, you have brought your claims to the attention of members of the Illinois legislature, which is the appropriate body to change the Illinois Educational Labor Relations Act.

For all of these reasons, we are declining your complaint.

Sincerely,

[signature]

Deputy Inspector General-Investigations

Now we see where the IELRB, the Illinois Appellate Court, and the OEIG are well organized to protect the interests of unions. I'm hopeful there will be little doubt that there is "fraudulent concealment" constantly going on in nearly every agency in Illinois by the end of this book.

I contacted other officials to try and expose the unions and the IELRB. I wrote to James M. Sullivan, the inspector general of the Chicago Board of Education. As I expected, Mr. Sullivan wrote back and told me, "Your complaint has been received. The issue cited in the complaint does not fall within the jurisdiction of the OIG to investigate." It was always interesting to me that when an agency told me it didn't have jurisdiction, they never mentioned an agency that did have jurisdiction.

I wrote to Governor Pat Quinn on November 17, 2009, but I

never heard from him. I also wrote to Karen Lewis on September 13, 2010. She was the president of the CTU and affiliated with the IFT. I complained to her about the CTU-IFT not providing fair representation to members. I never heard from her either.

I kept after Senator Duffy to launch an investigation into the antics of the IELRB because it had been hiding behind the fact that the state was acting illegally, and the IELRB seemed to agree with Ms. Doyle's interpretation of the law. However, Senator Duffy ignored several of my requests to look into wrongdoings in the IELRB and the seemingly confused OEIG. It was disheartening at best when he finally told me to stop contacting him, or he would, "turn me over to the authorities." I'm not sure what that meant, but it definitely told me Senator Duffy was no longer interested in my effort to stop unions from taking control of the government in which he served. I was beginning to see that state politicians were either afraid to launch investigations into questionable union activity or didn't know how. Or more likely, they refused to act because they saw it would be to their advantage to do whatever unions wanted when it came time to vote on union issues that would help unions prosper.

Based on the treatment I received from several state officials over at least five years, I recognized the Illinois government was a closed shop. It became crystal clear to me that if I were to have any chance to expose how unions were taking over Illinois government, I would have to turn my evidence over to the federal government.

CHAPTER 5

Involving the FBI

I decided to contact the FBI in Chicago. As will be seen, that decision was a good one. I called and told the agency I had a crime to report. A secretary connected me to an agent, Steve O' Reilly. He was very pleasant and seemed interested in my report. I told him what I had uncovered and that I had collected plenty of documentation that I would like to send him. We agreed we would start there. Since the evidence I sent Agent O' Reilly was rather cumbersome, I did not expect a quick reply. But sooner than I expected, he called, and we talked for nearly an hour.

The first thing he told me, and I will never forget it, was, "This case belongs in federal court." My spirits soared because his comment made me feel that my efforts to expose the unions and the crooked agencies, even the Illinois Appellate Court, was in the proper hands.

Agent O' Reilly and I spent a lot of time on the phone. Once he had to stop and go to a meeting and told me he would call me back. Although it was the next day, he did call, and we talked again for quite some time. I thought it important to find out what part of the evidence I submitted prompted him to tell me this should be a federal case. I think he thought a comment made within the IELRB ruling against me was very revealing. (See photo 10.)

"[r]estraining, coercing employees in the exercise of the rights guaranteed under this Act, provided that a labor organization or its agents shall commit an unfair labor practice under this paragraph in duty of fair representation cases only by intentional misconduct in representing employees under this Act." (emphasis added).

In Vaca v. Sipes, 386 U.S. 171 (1967), the Supreme Court held that a breach of the statutory duty of fair representation occurs only when a union's conduct toward a member of the collective bargaining unit is "arbitrary, discriminatory or in bad faith." The IELRB has adopted this standard in Community Consolidated School District No. 59, 1 PERI 1158, Case Nos. 85-CA-0007-C, 85-CB-0006-C (IELRB Opinion and Order, August 14, 1985), and Township High School District 214, 3 PERI 1121, Case Nos. 87-CA-0003-C, 87-CB-0002-C (IELRB Opinion and Order, November 10, 1987). In addition, the Illinois Educational Labor Relations Act requires that any breach of the duty of fair representation must be evidenced by intentional misconduct on the union's part. In Hoffman v. Lonza, Inc., 658 F.2d 519, 108 LRRM 2311 (7th Cir. 1981), the Court defined intentional misconduct as union action conducted in a "deliberate and severely hostile manner, or that it engaged in fraud, deceitful action or conduct." Therefore, under

MODIFIES FEDERAL LAW : IELRB RULING

Recall that I mentioned early in this book that the US Supreme Court ruling in *Vaca v. Sipes* essentially held that unions must back their constituents. They cannot act in an, "arbitrary, discriminatory or bad faith fashion." The document I sent agent O'Reilly pointed out that the IELRB stated that they had, "adopted this standard." That meant the IELRB accepted the *Vaca* ruling. It not only states that *Vaca* was adopted, it also states, "*In addition,* the Illinois Educational Labor Relations Act requires that any breach of the duty of fair representation must be evidenced by intentional misconduct on the union's part" (italics added for emphasis). Agent O' Reilly suggested I reread the IELRB ruling. He noted that statement by the IELRB actually modifies the US Supreme

Court decision. Agent O' Reilly said, "They can't do that." He explained that the words, "in addition," clearly show how the state modified federal law to benefit unions. Adding the "intentional misconduct" standard also completely changed the US Supreme Court ruling.

I now believe these illegal changes are what motivated Agent O'Reilly to tell me this case belonged in federal court. In fact, at that time he told me, "States must adhere to the supremacy doctrine afforded the Supreme Court." It now became obvious to me, thanks to Agent O'Reilly, that unions, the IELRB, and the Illinois Appellate Court have been ignoring this doctrine. They are in cahoots! These entities have become a well-oiled machine built to cheat union members out of the use of their dues. I thought back to what Keith Snyder wrote to my brother. Mr. Snyder, as you may recall, stated that "Unions had virtually a free hand to craft the standard they prefer," when it comes to unions providing funding and legal assistance to members whose rights have been infringed by unscrupulous employers.

By state law, the IELRB is required to publish the *Public Employee Reporter*. This periodical is supposed to publish factual summaries of fair representation cases brought before the IELRB. The review of my case (see the following summary) is tainted. I pointed this out to Agent O'Reilly. He agreed the summary is dishonest. He told me in one of our many sessions that "The state tries to be clever enough to stay under the radar." This summary is, obviously, one of those attempts to "stay under the radar."

> IELRB Exec. Dir.-Even assuming that union was exclusive representative...teacher failed to demonstrate that union engaged in intentional misconduct by refusing to fund or provide legal assistance in his age discrimination cause of action. Evidence indicated that union engaged several labor attorneys to review teacher's case before deciding to not pursue matter in court or provide legal defense grant. Moreover, teacher failed to establish his entitlement to representation under any collective bargaining agreement. AFT-IFT Jones 92-CB 7/01/92

The summary never mentioned that a federal judge ruled my case against high school district #211 meritorious. This omission fits snuggly with Agent O'Reilly's assertion that they stay under the radar. It is obvious the state and the IELRB, don't want the public to know that it is declining to fund and provide legal assistance to a union member, even though a federal judge declared his case should go to court.

Also note in the summary, the IELRB failed to mention my case was a First Amendment case. It referred to the case as an age discrimination case. Furthermore, the summary misrepresented the truth when it stated, "Evidence indicated that union engaged several labor attorneys to review teacher's case." In fact, union attorneys never read depositions in the case or even talked to any of my sixty-five witnesses. That was not even a respectful review. When the summary stated that I failed to establish entitlement to representation, it was just another dishonest statement designed to confuse readers. Obviously, I was a dues-paying member of the IFT-AFT-Local #211.

The *Public Employee Reporter* summary of my case showed what lengths the IELRB and the unions go to save unions money. They hide behind their own intentional misconduct standard, but that, too, is illegal. Federal Judge Cudahy of the 7th Circuit held in a case that "Arbitrary conduct is not limited to intentional misconduct. For example, to ignore a meritorious grievance or process it in a perfunctory fashion may be arbitrary." (*Vaca v. Sipes*; see also *Hines v. Anchor Motor Freight*). Judge Alesia in Chicago ruled that my case was meritorious and should proceed to court, but the summary in the *Public Employee Reporter* denied me that freedom. It should never have happened.

After numerous contacts with Agent O'Reilly, I asked him if the FBI would be filing charges against those people in Illinois helping to perpetuate union control of the state. He told me, "Our office is overwhelmed with cases. The FBI has a priority list of cases. The best way to get a case like yours moved up on the priority list is to get media exposure." I was disappointed because I thought my case should be at the top of the list. After all, it had so much to do with the well-being of the state. Illinois should not be under union control.

Agent O' Reilly mentioned that he thought it important to get the word out to union members that their dues were being wasted. So I set out to obtain media attention to accomplish that task.

I thought I had another good break in the case when I called ace *Chicago Tribune* reporter Jason Grotto. I was so happy when he almost immediately said he would come to my house and interview me about union activity. Jason interviewed me for nearly two hours and took all kinds of notes about the evidence. I remember so vividly him telling me, "This could be a series." That comment made my spirits soar because Jason had just written two classic series about taxes in Chicago. One article I found on the internet stated, "It seems that for years the Cook County assessor, Joe Berrios, overvalued low-priced properties while undervaluing high-priced ones. The deeply flawed system led to inequities in property taxes, punishing the poor and small businesses owners, while giving the wealthy unsanctioned tax breaks and lining the pockets of politically connected tax attorneys."

Jason wrote two articles about this tax situation. One was titled "Broken Bonds," and the other was titled "The Tax Divide." Jason's investigative report was so well detailed the publicity about the case cost Mr. Berrios his job. He was replaced by Fritz Kaegi. I was certain that this type of skillful investigative reporting was what Agent O' Reilly was telling me would be needed to move my case up on the FBI's priority list and help to expose how the unions began their quest to control Illinois government.

Jason Grotto interviewed me in November 2012. Years passed, and I didn't see any articles about unions written by him in the *Chicago Tribune*. Why, I don't know, but I guess I trusted Jason so much I didn't contact him until sometime in 2018. I found he had moved from the *Tribune* to a media outlet named *ProPublica*. I called him and asked why he had not published the in-depth report about unions that we had talked about. I reminded him that he had told me it could be a series of articles. I was shocked when he told me, "Unions can do whatever they want to do with their money." Jason had done a complete about-face after he interviewed me. I wondered if he had been influenced by the unions not to write a report. Or perhaps officials at the *Chicago Tribune* would not approve such an investigative report.

I continued to my attempts to get the media exposure Agent O'Reilly told me I needed. I had several contacts with Kristen McQueary, who was then the editorial page editor at the *Chicago Tribune.* At one time Kristen was quoted in her newspaper as saying, "Citizens complaints should not be universally brushed aside." I sent longtime reporter Ray Long the same evidence I sent to the FBI, but he never saw fit to expose the unions. I sent letters to the editors and wrote some op-eds, but all my writings and all my complaints about unions were ignored. Bruce Dold, editor-in-chief of the *Chicago Tribune* at the time, by not allowing meaningful publicity about the unions, didn't seem to stand behind his words, "The *Chicago Tribune* journalists dedicate themselves every day to investigating crucial issues." Evidently he didn't think unions robbing their members and taking over state government was a "crucial" issue.

A few short years after my contact with these journalists, an article appeared that asked, "Who is running Illinois government? It's not the administration. It's not the department heads. It's the public employee unions." I firmly believe that the *Chicago Tribune,* through its inaction about unions, helped tremendously to further union causes. The paper doesn't seem to meet the standards that legendary journalist Walter Cronkite suggested for the media: "One of the main duties of the press is monitoring the performance of government."

One of the last contacts I had with Agent O'Reilly was to tell him about Jason Grotto unwillingness to report on crooked unions. Agent O'Reilly retired, so I was left getting no help from state officials, the media, or from the FBI. That agency evidently determined that my report about unions would not be moved up on their priority list, no matter what I did. I was now in a catch-22. The FBI seemed to be telling me I must obtain media exposure, but most journalists ignored my pleas to expose what the unions were doing.

CHAPTER 6

Janus v. AFSCME

I was very discouraged about my lack of success in telling the story of what unions were doing to their members and to the people of Illinois. After all that the politicians, state agencies, the media, and the FBI had done to me, I decided my only choice was to wait for something that might renew my interest in telling what was still an untold story about union capers in Illinois.

Finally, in November 25, 2019, the *Chicago Tribune* editorial board published an article about the lawsuit union member Mark Janus filed against his union, the American Federation of State, County and Municipal Employees (AFSCME). The article caught my interest because it included phrases that told me, once again, unions had become very successful, since the Knapp case in Peoria, in doing whatever they needed to do to maintain their abilities to meet their two major goals: to pay union employees high salaries, and more important, to have funds to contribute to politicians the unions persuaded to always vote in their favor.

The article, "Illinois Lawmakers Try to Skirt the Impact of Janus: Why Gov. Pritzker Should Say No," focused on the fact that Janus's victory at the US Supreme Court limited the ability of public employee unions to collect mandatory dues.

EDITORIALS

Illinois lawmakers try to skirt the impact of Janus

WHY GOV. PRITZKER SHOULD SAY NO

Since June 27, 2018, when the U.S. Supreme Court limited the ability of public employees unions to collect mandatory dues, Mark Janus has been traveling the country on an information campaign.

Janus is the Springfield plaintiff who worked as a child support specialist for the state of Illinois. He declined to join the union when he was hired in 2007, but he still had to pay partial dues. The Supreme Court ruled in his favor last summer, deciding in a 5-4 opinion that mandatory dues collection from nonunion members violated their constitutional rights. Employees still are free to join unions and pay dues. But the justices said those who don't want to do so cannot be required to "subsidize the speech of other private speakers."

"States and public-sector unions may no longer extract agency fees from nonconsenting employees," Justice Samuel Alito Jr. wrote for the majority. "This procedure violates the First Amendment and cannot continue."

Since then, union-heavy states have been enacting laws to weaken the impact of the Janus decision. Which state probably is next to have such a law? You guessed it, Illinois.

Lawmakers during the fall veto session sent to Gov. J.B. Pritzker legislation that would make it easier for unions to recruit members and harder for employees to know their rights under Janus. Public employers — mostly governments — would be required to provide the names, addresses and contact information of their employees, including personal email addresses and cellphone numbers on file, directly to union bargaining units.

The legislation also severely limits the ability of employers to inform their workers about the choice to join a union or not.

"The Janus decision was about empowering individuals to make a choice of

Mark Janus poses for a photograph outside the State Capitol building in Springfield.

JOHN J. KIM/CHICAGO TRIBUNE 2018

what's right for them," Janus told us Thursday. "It puts people in charge of their membership, not politicians or a union steward. If the governor signs the bill, he's going to keep people in the dark."

For workers who don't want to join a union, the window to opt out would be shortened under the measure. And the bill protects unions from being forced to repay dues previously surrendered by workers like Janus.

That's the second phase of Janus' court battle — getting about $3,000 in dues returned to him from the American Federation of State, County and Municipal

Employees Council 31, now that the Supreme Court ruled the taking unconstitutional. "It's not about the taking unconstitutional. It's about righting the wrongs of the unions," Janus says.

"We're prepared to ultimately try to go back to the Supreme Court on this issue," says Janus attorney Jeffrey Schwab with the Liberty Justice Center. "We think it's important and doesn't just affect Mark. It affects everyone in Mark's position."

The Janus decision remains a liberating force for public sector employees who don't want to join a union, disagree

with a union's mission, or don't want their paychecks slashed to support political and other activity with which they disagree. Ultimately, accepting public service jobs in teaching or corrections or child welfare should not be predicated on joining a union. That's our view.

If Pritzker signs the bill, he will demonstrate once again who actually runs Illinois state government. It's not his administration. It's not the department heads. It's the public employees unions who represent more than 90% of the state workforce. They already have the power. Governor, why give them more?

The article at least gave me more encouragement about my chances to expose the tyranny unions were now able to spread around the state. Mark Janus, who lived in Springfield, worked as a child support specialist for the state of Illinois. He declined to join the union, but he still had to pay partial dues. He was represented in court by the Liberty Justice Center in Chicago and an organization named The Right to Work Legal Defense Foundation. The thing that got my attention was that Janus was able to get legal and financial help to file suit against AFSCME.

After reading the Janus article, I contacted the Liberty Justice Center for legal help. I thought it might be an organization I could use to file charges against the unions. I contacted Mailee Smith, who had done some work with the Liberty Justice Center. We communicated by email, and I asked if she could help get charges filed against the unions. She told me that "Fair representation cases are outside our expertise."

I asked her, "Why is it that you and your colleagues defended Mark Janus and his right not to have to pay union dues and won't fight for those union members who pay their dues and are having their rights infringed daily by unions that refuse to use union money to defend them?" There will be more about the Liberty Justice Center later.

The first thing that crossed my mind while reading the article about Mark Janus and his case against his union was that it didn't surprise me one bit that a big Illinois union would fight hard to keep dues revenue flowing. They were afraid other union members would opt out of paying dues and, therefore, put a dent in union finances. Again, I thought back to IFT lawyer Mildred Haggerty telling me, "The union can't afford to file a lawsuit for you." AFSCME had the funds to fight Janus all the way to the US Supreme Court, but the IFT in Chicago didn't have the funds to support me even after I obtained the ruling of a federal judge stating my case was meritorious. Anyone halfway interested in union power in Illinois could deduce that unions would spend money to fight any source that could limit their future income. Janus's case could do that, so AFSCME fought him. The union declined to support members who needed financial help to defend their rights because such action would endanger their coffers. Basically, any moves unions could make that ensured union employees lucrative paychecks and money to contribute to politicians who favored unions are what union leaders did. And they are still doing!

In the final decision in the Janus case, the Supreme Court held in a 5–4 vote that mandatory dues collection from nonunion members violated their constitutional rights. According to the article, union-heavy states had been enacting laws to weaken the impact of the Janus decision. The *Tribune* asked, "Which state probably is next to have such a law? You guessed it, Illinois." A real clue that shady state legislators supported unions because they contributed to their campaign coffers surfaced when lawmakers in the Illinois General Assembly sponsored bills to counteract the Janus ruling. The language in these bills would make it easier for unions to recruit members and harder for employees to know their rights under the Janus ruling. I believed the names of those state representatives and senators should be more widely publicized so citizens could see who in the General Assembly supported unions. Those names could come in handy if this great conspiracy ever came to light.

I immediately recalled that the labor lawyer I talked to told me that a well-organized conspiracy was underway and even told me the federal statutes that were being violated: conspiracy against rights and the deprivation of rights under color of law. I firmly believed then and now that those legislators who knowingly help to perpetuate union power should be indicted. Punishment under federal law is through incarceration or fines. I must say that FBI Agent Steve O'Reilly told me it was not illegal for politicians to sponsor and vote on such bills. What is wrong with politicians sponsoring such bills is how the unions accumulated enough money to pay off the lawmakers to vote in their favor in the first place.

In the Janus article, it can once again be seen how unions do their best to modify and manipulate federal laws. Bills were sent to Governor J. B. Pritzker, who was supported by unions during his campaign. The bills were aimed at dancing around federal law and were quickly enacted into law. While reading the article I realized what Agent O' Reilly told me about Illinois not adhering to the, "supremacy doctrine afforded the US Supreme Court," was true. Remember how the words "in addition" circumvented *Vaca*? Bills sent to Governor Pritzker were designed so unions would not have to adhere to federal law. There should be a law in Illinois that requires the state to adopt and then not tinker with US Supreme Court decisions. However, that is not going to happen in the near future because the people who could enact such a law are the ones who currently have the power to stop and benefit from it.

The Janus article is the one in which the *Chicago Tribune* asked, "Who actually runs Illinois state government? It's not the administration. It's not the department heads. It's the public employee unions." The article should have, in my view and the view of many of my colleagues and family members, sparked an investigation for the simple reason that unions should not be running Illinois government. It's like a silent insurrection has taken place, and no one cares to do anything about it. Rest assured the unions will run Illinois government until the federal government steps in and stops it.

Many people, especially those who oppose unions, thought the Janus victory would weaken unions as many people might realize they could enjoy negotiated union benefits without being a member. That didn't happen; union membership in Illinois is still very strong. And I believe there are many people in Illinois who think their unions will protect their rights if infringed. Unions are doing a good job of keeping their propensity not to do so a secret. Recall that Agent Steve O'Reilly thought it important to inform union members they are being cheated out of representation. But as he said, the unions, and those in government who protect them, are, "flying under the radar," and no one detects the systemic deception.

The reason the Janus article in the *Chicago Tribune* was so interesting to me was that Janus's union, the AMFSCME, used substantial money from its coffers to fight all the way to the US Supreme Court. They wanted the law to remain mandatory, meaning people had to pay dues if they wanted to benefit from union contracts. It is outrageous that, to this day, unions throughout Illinois won't file lawsuits for members whose rights are infringed for one reason or another. Of course, by not filing expensive lawsuits to protect members' rights, unions save big money, so they can fight battles like the one Janus brought their way. Essentially, Mark Janus's union fought him and had the money to do so because, in all likelihood, it did as other powerful unions in Illinois did—ignore requests for funding and legal assistance to defend members' rights.

Note: I do not have any evidence—as I do against the IFT, IEA, and the UAW—that AMFSCME chose not to file lawsuits on behalf of aggrieved members.

Incidentally, the governor before J. B. Pritzker, Bruce Rauner, was well aware that unions were controlling Illinois government. That knowledge was part of Mr. Rauner's reelection campaign. One of his campaign slogans was, "Drain the swamp in Springfield." This meant he wanted to change the culture in the General Assembly, where he knew union support was having a deleterious effect on government functioning to benefit its citizens. Bruce Rauner was governor when Janus first filed his lawsuit. He actually joined the lawsuit because to win it might have meant the weakening of union power in Illinois. Bruce Rauner lost to J. B. Pritzker primarily because the unions and Pritzker's wealth were too much to overcome. A friend told me, "If Rauner had taken a more aggressive approach and involved the feds and launched an investigation into how the unions became so powerful, he might have been reelected."

I thought a lot about what my friend said, and it could be true. If Governor Rauner had been able to publicize the illegal things unions were doing, the voters of Illinois would have been silly not to keep someone in office who could stop Illinois from becoming a dysfunctional, corrupt state.

Incidentally, just as I was preparing to send this manuscript to my publisher, the Illinois Policy Institute sent me more interesting material about how unions in Illinois treat their members. An article by Mailee Smith, who is the staff attorney and director of labor policy at the institute, reported that more than 38,000 state and local government workers across Illinois chose not to join or pay union dues since the US Supreme Court granted them that right in the Janus case. This 9 percent drop is a strong indication that unions are not in touch with their members. That should not surprise readers, considering my evidence about the behavior of unions in previous chapters. Interestingly, one union member, Benny Durbin, from Arthur, said, "I didn't like seeing the union give our money to political figures for their campaign funds. I don't like that at all. I think that's a waste of our own money."

A teacher from Glen Ellyn, Derrick Crenshaw, said, "My local union tried to tell me … that I wouldn't have any legal protection." It's too bad that Mr. Crenshaw didn't check that out as it is now known that he would have had to pay for legal help if he stayed in his union and needed legal protection.

The material from Mailee Smith showed how individuals can opt out of their unions. It also showed how unions have taken legal actions to make it more difficult to do so. Generally speaking, the Illinois Policy Institute does a good job trying to expose what unions do to cheat their members, but it does not have the authority to file lawsuits against Illinois unions.

CHAPTER 7

"If You See Something, Say Something"

During a great deal of the time I was trying to expose what the unions were doing to their members and the citizenry of Illinois, Patrick Fitzgerald was the US attorney in Chicago. He was the attorney who put former governor Rod Blagojevich in prison.

During his term in office, Mr. Fitzgerald was quoted in the *Chicago Tribune* speaking out about corruption in Chicago. I found his words quite profound. He said, "If you see something, say something. If you don't then you become part of the problem."

I had not been doing much to expose the tyrannical unions, but Mr. Fitzgerald's words inspired me to again do what I regarded as my civic duty. That was to use my substantial evidence and important words from Agent O'Reilly and contact people who might have courage enough to do what Mr. Fitzgerald suggested and speak out.

I hesitated to start contacting people again because I had done so several years before. In fact, I sent him my evidence on October 7, 2006. I received a letter from him dated November 2, 2006:

U.S. Department of Justice

United States Attorney
Northern District of Illinois

Everett McKinley Dirksen Building
219 S. Dearborn St., 5th Floor
Chicago, IL 60604

November 2, 2006

Norman Jones, Ed.D.
759 Silk Oak Lane
Crystal Lake, IL 60014

Dear Dr. Jones:

    This letter is to acknowledge receipt of your correspondence by this office dated October 7, 2006. Your complaint does not form the basis for any action by the United States Attorney's Office. Therefore, we cannot be of assistance to you regarding this matter.

    It is suggested that you direct any evidence of violations of federal law to the Federal Bureau of Investigation, 2111 West Roosevelt, Chicago, IL 60608-1128, for any action deemed appropriate.

                Very truly yours,

                PATRICK J. FITZGERALD
                United States Attorney

        By: **Screening Committee**

I was disappointed when I read that "Your complaint does not form the basis for any action by the United States Attorney's Office." Mr. Fitzgerald did refer me to the FBI, and I think that was when I began conversations with Steve O'Reilly.

At any rate, I decided to contact Congressman Dick Durbin, inform the senator of union antics in Illinois, and ask him to investigate the matter. The letter (photos 13 and 14) includes the fact that I had the support of the FBI in Chicago. I requested that Senator Durbin contact the US attorney and the FBI and find out what could be done to make unions in Illinois abide by federal statutes. I never heard from Senator Durbin.

Mr. Dick Durbin
U.S. Senator
230 S. Dearborn St.
Kluczynski Federal Bldg.
Suite 3892
Chicago, IL 60604

Dear Senator Durbin:

At the start of 2021 the *Chicago Tribune* reported that, "Unions have too firm of a grip on Illinois government." Later on the paper proclaimed, "Who actually runs Illinois government? It's not the administration. It's not the dept. heads. It's the public employee unions." I collected prima facie evidence regarding just how the unions managed to take over our government and submitted it to the FBI. Agent Steve O'Reilly called and told me, "This case belongs in federal court." We agreed that unions are taking in dues revenue, the life blood of union finances, and not using any of that money to file law suits for members who have had their civil rights infringed by unscrupulous employers. This plot allows unions to save money and keep their coffers healthy. Agent O'Reilly said, "Illinois is not abiding by the Supremacy Doctrine afforded the U.S. Supreme Court." That court has held that unions must "provide fair representation to members" and "cannot arbitrarily ignore meritorious cases." Since unions in Illinois are not adhering to Supreme Court decisions they are violating federal statutes.

In view of my report to you seen above I am requesting that you investigate this matter and, hopefully, help union members regain their right to be defended by unions. I sincerely hope that you believe that Illinois citizens deserve to have their elected government officials, such as you, provide honest services instead of being controlled by union leaders.

I urge you to look in to how the Illinois Educational Labor Relations Board (IELRB) "caters to unions" which is what I was told when I asked to file a charge there. Find out why the Illinois Appeals Court dismisses every fair representation case and rebukes the Supreme Court decisions that held unions must back their constituents. Find out how unions in Illinois force their members to pay for protection of their rights in order to save the unions money. Especially find out how Illinois law allows the State Attorney General to ignore corruption. There is much more to the union takeover that you can clean up with an honest effort on your part. I hope you will do, as your oath of office seems to obligate you to do, and that is uphold the laws of this state and this nation.

I will send your response to the FBI and the U.S. Attorney in Chicago. I would, of course, hope that you will contact these offices in an honest effort to stop the union takeover of Illinois government. I hope to hear from you soon and thank you for your interest in making Illinois a more functional state.

Respectfully,

Norman Jones

Dr. Norman Jones   Crystal Lake, IL

I became suspicious when Senator Durbin did not give me the courtesy of a reply, especially since I was reporting what looked like

criminal activity in Illinois. I always believed that elected officials owe
it to their constituents to do what their oaths require them to do, which
is, "To uphold the laws of this state and this nation." I was suspicious
because I thought that just maybe Senator Durbin was beholden to
unions. After all, I had discovered many politically connected people
in Illinois were catering to unions. *Bingo!* I checked Senator Durbin's
website and found out that during his long term in office, which started
in 1996, he was able to obtain money from about 140 unions. You can
see in the partial chart that follows (photo 15) that some of the unions
I have mentioned in this book, including the IFT, AFT, AFSCME,
and the NEA, are contributors to keeping Senator Durbin in office.
Understand that these contributions are not illegal. However, the
question I was asking top officials to investigate was how the unions
accumulate the money they contribute to the campaigns of politicians
who do favors for them.

Dick Durbin (D): Contributions from Unions

American Fedn of St/Cnty/Munic Employees (/pac/American_Fedn_of_St--Cnty--Munic_Employees)	101000.00
Air Line Pilots Assn (/pac/Air_Line_Pilots_Assn)	101000.00
National Education Assn (/pac/National_Education_Assn)	99800.00
United Transportation Union (/pac/United_Transportation_Union)	96356.00
Teamsters Union (/pac/Teamsters_Union)	88000.00
AFL-CIO (/pac/AFL-CIO)	86354.00
Communications Workers of America (/pac/Communications_Workers_of_America)	81000.00
American Federation of Teachers (/pac/American_Federation_of_Teachers)	80000.00
National Assn of Letter Carriers (/pac/National_Assn_of_Letter_Carriers)	74000.00
United Food & Commercial Workers Union (/pac/United_Food_%26_Commercial_Workers_Union)	71700.00
Carpenters & Joiners Union (/pac/Carpenters_%26_Joiners_Union)	70500.00

It should be obvious that the reason Senator Durbin didn't reply to me or launch an investigation into Illinois unions is because such action could cost him tons of money usually contributed by the unions in the state. Sometimes people in Illinois label this, "Pay to play."

After being ignored by Senator Durbin, I wondered what method of speaking Patrick Fitzgerald had when he told people to speak up if they saw something. It was discouraging at best to have a congressman ignore my speaking out, so I had to try another way. I thought maybe that many Illinois politicians had become aware of Mr. Fitzgerald's urging for people to speak out about corruption, so I decided to go back to Illinois lawmakers and ask for an investigation. I wrote a lengthy letter to newly elected State Representative Suzanne Ness, explaining the situation with unions and requesting that she contact the FBI and launch an investigation. She replied, "I have found many areas of inefficiency, a lack of accountability and conflicts of interest and I plan to address those three things either through legislation, subject matter hearings or amending current legislation." Notice, however, that she avoided mentioning contacting the FBI.

I responded to Representative Ness in an article (photo 16) I got published in the *Northwest Herald,* located in Crystal Lake, Illinois. I noted that "When will our state legislators learn that trying to reform a government that is controlled by unions will not happen through state legislation? Some brave politician is going to have to file a report with the federal government if reform is going to happen."

Northwest Herald / NWHerald.com • Saturday, Sep 25, 2021 | NORTHWEST HERALD

Courage needed among legislators

To the Editor:

In the past two decades, I have contacted state legislators representing McHenry County and requested that they launch an investigation into how unions have taken control of Illinois government. One response was, "This case is too old and nothing can be done."

There is little bravery and courage among legislators to do anything about the corruption that torments our state. I recently contacted state Rep. Suzanne Ness and asked her to contact the FBI and show how unions are, indeed, running state government. I sent her information, but she didn't file a report with the FBI. She told me, "I have found many areas of inefficiency, a lack of accountability and conflicts of interest and I plan to address those three things either through legislation, subject matter hearings or amending current legislation."

When will our state legislators learn that trying to reform a government that is controlled by unions will not happen through state legislation? Some brave politician is going to have to file a report with the federal government if reform in going to happen.

A recent editorial in the Northwest Herald from the Effingham Daily News titled, "Another Legislature ethics placebo for the people of Illinois" was one of the best I have read that shows the games being played in Springfield. The editorial stated, "The Illinois General Assembly is a master of approving phony reform bills" and that most bills are "empty shells devoid of substantive, positive changes." Not so surprising was the comment, "Obviously, lawmakers of this scandal-ridden state have shown they want nothing to do with changes that would undermine their ability to profit one way or another from their legislative duties."

Norman Jones
Crystal Lake

Mrs. Melinda Bush of Grayslake (D) became a state senator from my area, so I decided to contact her. During this attempt, I was able to get another article published in the local paper, and I mentioned her (photo 17). I noted that in Mrs. Bush's campaign, she proclaimed, "It's time to deal with the culture in Springfield."

Unions and the culture in Springfield

To the Editor:

Candidates for state offices now are running TV ads proclaiming they want to clean up Springfield. Current state Sen. Melinda Bush, D-Grayslake, recently proclaimed, "It is time to deal with the culture in Springfield." It is a known fact that Illinois government is dysfunctional and that unions are controlling state government.

I sent Sen. Bush a plethora of evidence showing the moves unions have made to enhance their takeover. I never heard from her. Years ago, I sent union corruption evidence to McHenry County state legislators. Sen. Pam Althoff and Rep. Barb Wheeler agreed, "This case is too old. Nothing can be done."

State Rep. Jack Franks told me, "File your own lawsuit. When you become a pauper, then the state can help you."

It is clear elected officials will have to delve into just how unions have obtained the power to run Illinois government and take action to stop it.

Attitudes like that of Bush, Althoff, Wheeler and Franks help to perpetuate corruption in Illinois. Promises to clean up Springfield will go unfulfilled unless we elect people with courage and bravery who will launch investigations designed to expose how the unions maintain government control.

Such control obviously is illegal; and appeals need to be made to the federal government for help in ridding Illinois of such tyranny. I did send my evidence to the FBI and the U.S. Attorney's Office. The FBI told me, "This case belongs in federal court."

The agency urged me to obtain media exposure, as this helps to move cases up on the FBI priority list. Newly elected officials will need to do all they can to get media exposure to, hopefully, motivate the feds to take action.

Legendary journalist Walter Cronkite once said, "One of the main duties of the press is monitoring the performance of government."

If the media and honest politicians work together, maybe Illinois can rid itself of a dysfunctional government.

Norman Jones
Crystal Lake

In trying to follow what Patrick Fitzgerald said, I sent Senator Bush myriad evidence showing the moves unions had made to enhance their takeovers. I thought she might be able to use it to "deal with the culture in Springfield." I never heard from Senator Bush.

Suspicious again, I checked Senator Bush's website, as I had with Senator Durbin. Sure enough, I found her also to be involved with unions in Illinois. She received $50,000 from AFSCCME, $47,500 from the IEA, $43,700 from the Lake County Federation of Teachers, $39,000 from the IFT, $57,800 from the International Brotherhood of Electrical Workers (IBEW), and $39,500 from the Midwest Region

Laborers. Again, these donations to politicians are not illegal. Unions have the right to work to get people who might help them elected in to offices just as we, as voters, have the right to vote for those who share our views on things. My complaint to Senator Bush was about how the unions accumulate the money, and as stated many times herein, they do so by not using the dues members pay to protect member rights.

After not hearing from Senator Bush, I contacted a new state representative by the name of Martin McLaughlin. I mentioned to him in an email how the unions were cheating their members by not filing lawsuits to protect them when harassed. I pointed out how such skullduggery helped unions save money, allowing them to contribute to politicians who favored unions and to pay union employees high if not outrageous salaries. He sent me an email and made a very astute observation: "I do believe that public labor unions influence on Democratic legislation is one of the great obstacles to be overcome." I thought I had hit the jackpot and finally found a courageous Illinois lawmaker who might possibly launch an investigation into how the unions enabled themselves to run Illinois government. I quickly sent him my packet of evidence. But I was again disappointed; I never heard from him again. It remained amazing to me to know numerous state lawmakers were aware of union capers but didn't have the courage to stop them.

I was able to speak out in the local paper (photo 18). I hoped the article would inspire someone with the authority to challenge the unions to do so.

Because of Springfield cowardice, unions running state govern⸱ent

To the Editor:

Former U.S. District Attorney Patrick Fitzgerald urged citizens to report suspicious behavior. He said, "If you see something, say something."

Since then, a major media outlet reported, "Who actually runs Illinois government? It's not the administration. It's not the department heads. It's the public employee unions."

Two years ago, I "said something" to McHenry County legislators about how I had written documentation that showed how unions take in dues and revenue and never use that money to defend the civil rights of members. This defense is mandated by two U.S. Supreme Court decisions, but the state officers ignored the law. By not filing lawsuits, unions save a great amount of money. The money is being used to infiltrate state government to the point that unions control what happens in Springfield.

I sent my documentation to the FBI.

It showed how unions now control decisions in state courts, boards and important offices. An FBI spokesman told me, "This case belongs in federal court," and noted, "The state must adhere to the Supremacy Doctrine afforded the Supreme Court."

Recently, I communicated with state Rep. Martin McLaughlin. He said, "I do believe that public labor union's influ-⸱⸱⸱ on Democratic legislation is one of the g⸱⸱⸱ ⸱bstacles that needs to be overcome." I sent him my evidence and asked him to take action against the unions. I never heard from him. I sent the evidence to state Sen. Melinda Bush, who once stated, "It's time to deal with the culture in Springfield," but she never replied. It seems legislators understand that it would be a waste of their time to appeal to state officials being controlled by unions. Rather, it is imperative they "say something" to federal authorities, since a corrupt state government is not going to investigate itself. This plea to the feds will take courage and bravery that seems to have been replaced by cowardice that prevents officials from providing honest services to citizens. Exposing how unions gained control of Illinois government should be revealed if for no other reason than this: Secrecy is the enemy of democracy.

Norman Jones
Crystal Lake

Since I had not done so, I now felt it was important to contact my McHenry County state's attorney, Patrick Kenneally. I sent him this message in an email:

Dear Mr. Kenneally,

I would like to know what is being done about unions taking over Illinois government. As I am sure you know, the *Chicago Tribune* reported some time ago that, "Unions are running Illinois government." This has to be illegal and I would like to know if such tyranny is being addressed by state officials?" Thank you.

Respectfully,
Dr. Norman Jones

Mr. Kenneally's reply was unbelievable and told me a lot about Illinois government. For all of you reading his message, I would think you would be taken aback by such a response from a state's attorney. His reply is shown here in its entirety:

Dear Mr. Jones,

    The short answer is that very little is being done to counteract the influence of unions in Illinois. Rather, just the opposite. Unions are being supported, financed, and encouraged by State officials. These days, school unions are some of the worst actors, driving up property taxes with their exorbitant demands and pushing highly contentious and controversial "lesson plans" on children. The simple answer is to do in Illinois what they did in Wisconsin, which is to prohibit public unions so that they don't turn into a fourth estate like they have in Illinois and use their influence to undermine majority rule and opinion.

    As you may know, unions are protected under both federal and state law. While, in my opinion, much of their activity is counterproductive and causes more problems than it fixes, nothing they are doing is illegal *per se*. As such, there is very little I or any other official can who is not in the legislature can do address many of the concerns that you and I may share.

Patrick Kenneally
McHenry County State's Attorney
2200 North Seminary Avenue, Suite 150
Woodstock, IL 60098
815-334-4159

Mr. Kenneally admitted that "very little is being done to counteract the influence of unions in Illinois." Shockingly, he also admitted that "Unions are being supported, financed and encouraged by State officials." I found it interesting that he stated, "As you may know, unions are protected under both federal and state law." And he went on to say, "Nothing they are doing is illegal, per se." That is not what the FBI told me, and for the McHenry County state's attorney to make such a comment should convince anyone reading this report that FBI Agent Steve O'Reilly was right in that unions are clever in their ability to fly under the radar. Mr. Kenneally belief that nothing unions were doing was illegal proved to me that, as Agent O'Reilly had told me, the case against unions, "belongs in federal court," and that Illinois was not abiding by the supremacy doctrine afforded by the US Supreme Court. Agent O'Reilly had noted it was illegal to modify and change supreme court decisions. But unions were able to craft their own laws, and by using the words, "In addition to," when they wanted to change the language in *Vaca*, it made the standard for fair representation much higher for union members to overcome when fighting for their rights to use union lawyers and funding.

Remember also how the IELRB submitted a tainted summary in the *Illinois Employee Reporter* about my case, which helped this sleazy board avoid being detected as a state agency that, as it admits, "caters" to unions. And don't forget it is crystal clear that the IELRB dismisses all fair representation cases, and the Illinois Appellate Court held that unions have no obligation to fund lawsuits for their members. Of course, this rebukes controlling federal law.

Mr. Kenneally was dead wrong when he said unions were not doing anything illegal. How could it be legal for unions to control a state government? Either Mr. Kenneally was afraid to dig into the case, or he had been duped into believing that unions had done nothing illegal in taking control of Springfield. Obviously, there needs to be a closer working relationship between Illinois government and federal government. The two must design a system that makes the sharing of information easier and quicker. It is sad for the people of Illinois that help depended in part on my ability to move my case up the FBI's priority list. He said, "If that happens, then we might be able to get something done."

In case you haven't yet figured out, the purpose of this book is, hopefully, to expose the unions. As I stated earlier, I feel as though I am caught in a catch-22. I know I have proven the unions and a state government indebted to them are ruining Illinois, but I have not yet been able to persuade the federal government to take action to stop the charade, the scam, the tyranny going on in the state. It is a cinch that the state is not going to investigate itself, so if the feds don't get involved, union members will continue to be pawns of union power.

After Patrick Fitzgerald urged citizens to speak out about corruption, I kept thinking about ways to do so. I thought getting comments about the unions and state government being in cahoots published in a newspaper would be an effective way to speak out. Scott Holland is a good writer and writes a classy column about state government in the *Northwest Herald,* which has a home office in Crystal Lake. I sent him an email, and he quickly replied. In my message to him I mentioned that an FBI agent urged me to get media exposure about the unions and government having a love affair. I told him, "I think you could be instrumental in exposing the illegal stuff unions do by writing about their capers in your column." I mentioned that I would be sending him my packet of evidence and that I would be grateful for his help.

I was inspired to send him material because in our communications he said, "I have concerns about the influence of unions on state government." I was pleased to read that comment because I thought I had a journalist who would follow the thinking of legendary journalist Walter Cronkite, who said, "One of the main duties of the press is monitoring the performance of government." I sent Mr. Holland the same material I sent the FBI and told him, "I think we can work together to expose unions to the extent the FBI and the US district attorney will see fit to prosecute them and eventually make Illinois a more functional state in which to live." I never heard from Mr. Holland again. And as of this writing, he has not written any article about unions and their firm grip on Illinois government. I began to wonder if journalists were afraid to write about the powerful unions in Illinois, or perhaps they, too, were beholden to them.

About this time I began to think that it seemed unfair that the FBI placed the onus on citizens trying to do their civic duty to get media exposure for obvious crimes. Nevertheless, I tried again to get exposure and wrote an op-ed to the *Chicago Tribune.* I would be pleased if I could get similar coverage as Tonya Exum did when she spoke out about her union, which was the powerful UAW. She stated in her op-ed, "Don't expect your union to have your back." Photos 20 and 21 is a copy of the op-ed I sent to the *Chicago Tribune*. It didn't get published. I could not understand how Tonya could get her complaint about unions into a *Tribune* op-ed, but I got crickets from the *Tribune*.

How Illinois Unions Have Taken Over State Government

Early in 2020 the *Tribune* reported that, "Unions have too firm of a grip on state government" and asked, "Who actually runs Illinois government? It's not the administration. It's not the dept. heads. It's the public employees unions." I believe union control started over thirty years ago...in Peoria. Teacher Terry Knapp, a member of the IFT-AFT, won a First Amendment case against the Peoria school board, but damages awarded him mostly went to union lawyers. Charging the union member legal fees rebuked U.S. Supreme Court decisions. (*Vaca vs. Sipes and Hines vs. Anchor Motor Freight*) These decisions held that unions must use union funds to defend member rights. After this 1984 case, unions decided they could not stay solvent and pay for costly law suits. They proceeded to infiltrate state agencies so they could influence decisions that affected union solvency.

Recently, the *Tribune* gave clues that Illinois unions were not funding law suits. Pregnant teachers in the CTU who were being harassed by a principal had to use the U. S. Dept. of Justice to defend their rights. Another union member reported that she had to "fend" for herself when harassed and another IFT-AFT member had his case ignored even though a federal judge ruled his case meritorious.

After former U.S. Attorney Patrick Fitzgerald said: "If you see something, say something." I, as a former IFT-AFT member, watched union actions closely. I decided to accumulate evidence concerning what seemed to be a union plot to save money by not funding law suits. For me, there was no better place to speak out than in the *Chicago Tribune*. Here, in this op-ed, is some of the evidence I uncovered that shows how unions have taken control of state government. All evidence is documented in writing:

- The IELRB dismisses all fair representation cases thereby saving unions tons of money. In alarming documentation, the IELRB admits unions have the ability to "craft" their own laws regarding union behavior.

*The Illinois Appeals Court, in rebuking federal law, has held that, "Unions have no obligation to provide funding" to defend member rights.

* The Office of the Executive Inspector General has stated in a letter that, "In regard to labor relations, state laws take precedence over federal labor laws."

• I provided testimony before a House Labor Committee that informed legislators about how unions are ignoring member rights. My state rep sponsored a bill that would bring Illinois labor law in line with the federal statutes, but it was tabled.

• The IELRB is required by law to publish a summary of all fair representation cases. I have it documented that many of these summaries are deceitful and an attempt to hide from the public and authorities the truth about dismissed cases. This board has admitted it "caters" to unions.

• Lisa Madigan sent me an unsolicited Whistleblower Intake Form after I had asked 114 members of the General Assembly to investigate the union plot. She dismissed my allegations.

• Clearly, there is a conspiracy involving many members of the General Assembly, the union leadership, state agencies and even the courts to help unions save money. Money is power in Illinois and the union wealth has reached a level where it is now controlling Illinois government.

Unions are unlawfully profiting from union dues and are ignoring two important federal statutes. They are *CONSPIRACY AGAINST RIGHTS* AND *DEPRIVATION of RIGHTS UNDER COLOR of LAW*. It is hoped that this op-ed will inspire the *Tribune* to investigate and expose the union conspiracy and motivate authorities to take the proper legal action to rid Illinois of such corruption.

(Dr. Norman Jones is a retired teacher. He has taught graduate courses in Counseling and Human Development for Secondary School Administrators at Northeastern Illinois University and Roosevelt University. He has published four books the last of which is titled *Main St. vs. Wall St.: Wake-up Calls for America's Leaders.*)

I was getting increasingly discouraged. I seemed to be finding myself in a position where I needed to take a shotgun approach and contact anyone who might be in a position to use my material and expose the cowardly unions and misguided state government.

I wrote to the editor in chief of the *Chicago Tribune,* Bruce Dold. He sent me an email and said, "We can't help you." I wrote to some of Chicago's best-known investigative reporters. Carol Marin of NBC-TV 5 did respond but gave an excuse not to help me. Chuck Goudie of ABC-TV 7 did not even respond. Chris Coffey, also of NBC-TV 5, emailed me and said he, "Would pass the case on to others." I wrote to George Papajohn, who at the time was in charge of investigations at the *Chicago Tribune,* who merely told me, "I suggest you find another reporter." I wrote and called the office of Bruce Rauner, who was governor at the time. He had, as mentioned, joined the Mark Janus lawsuit. He lost the governorship to J. B. Pritzker.

I believed in what Patrick Fitzgerald urged citizens to do. And even long after he left office, I contacted the US attorneys who followed him. Zach Fardon and John Lausch Jr. always responded, but neither took action. I did get one somewhat encouraging letter from who was, and still is as of this writing, the FBI special agent in charge, Emerson Buie Jr. I always had in the back of my mind the idea that the FBI should be doing something to help the people of Illinois come out from under union control. Steve O'Reilly had told me he knew Patrick Fitzgerald's office had been informed about the ugly situation about the unions and the shady things they were doing to maintain their power. Mr. Buie's response is shown in photo 22.

It continues to bother me that both the US attorney and the FBI in Chicago are well aware of the union takeover of government in Illinois. But their lack of legal action against those who are perpetuating the situation, which has become a giant conspiracy, seems to betray the people of Illinois. I did receive one other letter from Mr. Fitzgerald's office. It seemed to indicate that if any action were to be taken by his office, it would have to be requested by the FBI. (See photo 22.)

Dr. Norman Jones

U. S. Department of Justice
Federal Bureau of Investigation

In reply, please refer to
File no.

FBI Chicago Division
2111 W. Roosevelt Road
Chicago, IL 60608

Attention: Dr. Norman Jones
759 Silk Oak Lane
Crystal Lake, IL 60014

RE: Two letters submitted to the FBI Chicago

Dear Dr. Jones:

Thank you for submitting the two letters dated 5/29/2020 and 7/13/2020 respectively, regarding "The Undeniable Truth About How Illinois Unions Built Power To Run State Government" and "An Update On the Evidence That Reveals How Unions In Illinois Have Taken Over State Government." It is very much appreciated when citizens report their observations and suspicions to the FBI. With regards to the content of the letters, the FBI is not in a position at this time to pursue the allegations any further, but will keep the letters and their contents for future reference. If you develop more recent information regarding the topics you have referenced in the letters, please don't hesitate to contact the FBI.

Respectfully Yours,
Emerson J. Buie, Jr.
Special Agent in Chicago

At one point in my investigation, I called the US Department of Justice in Washington, DC. I began explaining the purpose of my call to a woman on the phone. After a few minutes, she said, "Have a nice day," and hung up.

CHAPTER 8

Unions and the Law

I was proud that I had the motivation to find out how a union could ignore the fact that a union member—me—could convince a federal judge to rule the union member's case meritorious and should proceed to court. I was also proud that I had the wherewithal to contact the FBI and find out where I stood in relation to the union cheating me out of representation. It was very gratifying to hear Agent O'Reilly tell me, "This case belongs in federal court." Since I had struck out in my attempts to expose the situation, I decided one last thing I could do was research the law regarding what unions could do and could not do. I had often heard that we are a nation of laws. Therefore, I decided a chapter was needed to at least make the laws that control union behavior known so that if some brave soul in authority is inclined to do something about it, he or she can make use of what I found about unions and the law.

When the Illinois Appellate Court ruled that unions had no duty to provide funding and legal assistance to an aggrieved member, it was the impetus for me to prove herein, with cited laws, that the ruling rebukes federal law. Both the IELRB and the Illinois Appellate Court undermine federal law when they hold that unions have no obligation to defend the rights of their members.

Insofar as the law applies to unions, both the IELRB and the Illinois Appellate Court used state laws to get my case dismissed. This is not surprising when we go back to the letter from Janet Doyle, an assistant in the office of the state inspector general, and read that in matters regarding labor relations, state laws take precedence over federal laws.

My research regarding laws that govern unions and members will, hopefully, someday be used against unions to make them abide by precedent law. My search revealed this case wording and made it clear that Ms. Doyle misspoke about controlling laws. It was brought forth in *Peterson v. Air Lines Pilot Assoc. Intern,* 759 F. 2nd, 1161, C.A. (4) N.C. 1985: "A fair representation cause of action is governed exclusively by Federal law." That federal law certainly shows that Ms. Doyle and the state of Illinois are, as Agent O'Reilly indicated, manipulating and actually changing federal laws in order to cater to unions.

My research under mostly the heading "fair representation" showed that the latitude of unions to provide or not provide fair representation to members has been narrowed by the courts in the last few years. These updated decisions now favor dues-paying members. Union members now have a reasonable chance to prevail against their unions. Of course, these newly enacted federal laws make the "intentional misconduct standard" that the IELRB and the Illinois Appellate Court used to dismiss all cases now irrelevant.

Interestingly, I found a federal case ruled on in 1984 in which a union member who prevailed in a summary judgment attempt by his employer, "must be awarded attorney fees." It was the case of *Rosario v. Amalgamated Ladies Garment Cutters Union, Local 10, I.L. G. W.U.,* 749 F. 2nd, 1,100: "Union members had already prevailed through a summary declaratory judgment ... and this did not preclude an award of attorney fees to members." Remember that in my case against my school district, I had prevailed in the district's attempt to get my case dismissed. And don't forget, the union still defied federal law and would not take my case. As I pointed out earlier, the IFT lawyers not taking on my case were engaging themselves in the ongoing plot to save the union money.

Another federal case I found tightened the rules so unions can no longer ignore member complaints about their rights being infringed. The case revealed that "A union member could prevail in damages 'even' if it is uncertain whether employee would have prevailed in his claim against employer" (*Karahalios v. Defense Language Institute Foreign Language Center, Presido of Monterey,* 613 F. Supp. 440-1984). This case shows that just because the union may believe the case may be difficult to prove is no reason, based on current federal decisions, to deny a union member fair representation.

It is important to keep in mind when reading this review of cases pertinent to union behavior that unions cannot arbitrarily ignore a case; they must act in good faith when employees ask for help when their employers try to infringe on their rights. One judge noted that in *Hines v. Anchor Motor Freight,* "Hines reaffirms the proposition that merely 'arbitrary' conduct by a union is a clear basis of liability." Also in *Hines,* the US Supreme Court held that a union could be liable if it, "inadequately investigates, a grievance by overlooking critical facts or witnesses." I mention this because the union lawyers never talked to any of the sixty-five witnesses I had in my case against high school district #211. The union has to be guilty of inadequately investigating when it didn't talk to witnesses or even read depositions.

Vaca v. Sipes was a very important precedent in my case. It is the one that Agent Steve O'Reilly pointed out to me that was being modified, which is illegal. The IELRB stated in dismissing my case that this board had "adopted" *Vaca* but then modified the law by stating, "In addition, the Illinois Educational Labor Relations Act requires that any breach of the duty of fair representation must be evidenced by intentional misconduct on the union's part. The courts have defined intentional misconduct as union action conducted in a deliberate and severely hostile manner or that it engaged in fraud, deceitful action or conduct."

I reported to the FBI and the US attorney in Chicago that Agent O'Reilly, not only told me the state was deliberately modifying a federal statute (*Vaca*), but also that it was not abiding by the supremacy doctrine afforded by the US Supreme Court. As shown in previous chapters, altering *Vaca* gave unions an advantage. They should not, by federal law, be allowed to take advantage of their ill-conceived, deceitful changes. It is absolutely un-American that the FBI and the US attorney have, until now, permitted unions in Illinois to allow state-concocted laws, crafted by unions, help them to cheat their members by taking in dues revenue and not using that money to follow the law regarding fair representation of members. With such inaction by the federal government in Chicago, it should be clear to any reasonable person that the federal agencies in Chicago help to perpetuate the power of unions in the state. It is disgraceful and should be revisited.

Although I do not have a law degree, I have learned a great deal about labor law, fair representation, and laws governing unions as I moved forward with my civic duty to do what Agent O'Reilly urged me to do—expose the unions and politicians who do their best to keep the unions from being exposed. The politicians, by turning a blind eye to the union conspiracy, benefit in terms of donations to their campaign coffers.

One thing I was elated to learn about is what speech is protected in a First Amendment case like the one I filed against the school district. The courts have held that protected speech must be of public concern. Speech that is personal in nature will not survive in court. The IFT lawyers tried to show that my speech was personal, but Judge Alesia sabotaged that notion when he stated in my case that "Jones's speech is clearly protected by the First Amendment as it focuses on the improvement of communication in our schools in order to ensure better quality education." Judge Alesia made it clear in his decision that "A jury might infer that Jones was retaliated against and that his evaluations declined about the time he was speaking out." He noted that a jury might infer that the declining evaluations, "Did not result from the reasons cited by the defendants, but rather from certain statements made by Jones which were offensive to the defendants." Judge Alesia continued, "The court considers the timing of Jones' receipt of bad evaluations to support plaintiff's theory" of my First Amendment claim. Judge Alesia ruled that "material facts" exist in the case. That statement fits in well with the just-mentioned Supreme Court case where the court ruled a union can be held liable if it inadequately investigates a grievance by overlooking critical facts or witnesses.

People in Chicago might bend over laughing when considering how the IFT tried to get around representing me. Remember that union lawyer Mildred Haggerty told me the union didn't have the money to file a lawsuit for me. Most everyone knows that the IFT-AFT and the CTU are very rich. That the union doesn't have money to support a case that a federal judge already found meritorious is ridiculous. The excuse doesn't hold water because it rebukes standing federal law. One case held, "Despite union's plea of poverty, district court, in awarding union member back pay, attorney fees and costs, properly found no substantial evidence indicating that allowance of such sums would jeopardize union's stability (*Rollison v. Hotel, Motel, Restaurant and Const. Camp Emp. Local 879 AFL-CIO,* 677 F. 2nd. 741 [1982]).

It is again un-American that the FBI and the US attorney fail to recognize the excuses unions give to flaunt federal law. By not enforcing the law about unions pleading poverty, these agencies essentially give the unions a license to steal from their members.

I found out that the intentional misconduct standard to prove a union guilty of an unfair labor violation is now out of date. Federal judge Cudahy included this opinion when he stated, "Something less than scienter (or intentionally) seems to be sufficient given the courts' decision in Gateway." Moreover, he noted that "Egregious behavior (not necessarily intentional) (Robesky, 573 F. 2nd at 1089 91) apparently constitutes the triggering level of conduct for a union to breach of its duty of fair representation without doing violence to the decisions of this court and other federal courts." It may indeed be construed by a federal court that it is egregious or conspicuously bad behavior for a union to deny fair representation to a member when that member has already established the case in federal court that material facts exist. Alas, when the court discovers the union lawyers never even talked to witnesses, and so on, it might be considered reckless disregard for the rights of a union worker.

If an honest review of the above cited cases is undertaken by someone with the authority to do so, it should inspire charges against union leadership and against people in government agencies who persist in devising a pattern of deceit, obstruction of justice, and aiding and abetting unions. There is no doubt that complete avoidance of these now-listed laws gives unions unlimited power. The *Chicago Tribune* itself could help by paying more attention to the laws that unions break every day. Exposure of the unions' illegal actions could eventually lead to eliminating those forces that currently are making Illinois a dysfunctional state.

An intriguing editorial about Illinois attorney general Lisa Madigan appeared in the *Chicago Tribune* (photo 23). It focused on her confirmation that she was going to run for reelection in 2018. The article is titled, "Illinois' Incomplete Attorney General." The subtitle is, "Lisa Madigan Says She'll Run Again. If Only She Had a Stronger Record Fighting Illinois Corruption." It got my attention.

Illinois' incomplete attorney general

Lisa Madigan says she'll run again. If only she had a stronger record fighting Illinois corruption.

M. SPENCER GREEN/AP 2014

Illinois Attorney General Lisa Madigan

With little fanfare, Attorney General Lisa Madigan recently confirmed she plans to run for re-election in 2018. If she wins and completes another term, she will finish her 20th year on the job.

Twenty years is a long time. The year Madigan was elected attorney general, the trajectory for Illinois governance bent skyward. Citizens felt more confident in state leadership after a felony-prone governor, George Ryan, departed.

Democrats assumed control of the legislature and governor's office with a new governor, Rod Blagojevich, vowing to reform a government nakedly intertwined with contract steering, bribery, patronage, obstruction, lying and money-grubbing. Nearly 80 defendants, including Ryan himself, were convicted as part of an exhaustive federal probe that put a focus on the Illinois culture of political sleaze.

Illinois voters swept Madigan into office along with dozens of reform-minded lawmakers on promises they would clean house. Ethics topped the list of concerns for voters. Trust. Not budgets or pensions or debt. Madigan, who was then a 36-year-old first-term state senator, spent most of her campaign reassuring voters the attorney general role would not create conflicts of interest with her father, Michael Madi-

gan, now the longest-serving House speaker in the nation.

"All too often in recent years we have seen our current attorney general sit on the sidelines in the face of mounting evidence of government corruption," Lisa Madigan wrote to the Tribune as a candidate in 2002.

On the campaign trail, she said allegations of wrongdoing "must be investigated, no matter if they involve Democrats, Republicans or even my father."

But somewhere along the path to reform, Attorney General Madigan dimmed the lights. She stood in the shadows as other officials took heat for exposing clout and crimes among clouted government insiders. She quietly refocused her mission: heavy on consumer advocacy, easy on

corruption-busting.

Dozens more elected officials and their cohorts have been convicted on corruption charges at the local, county and state levels. Scandals come and go. Madigan, the state's top law enforcement official, has been glued to the sidelines, often citing the statutory limitations of her office to prosecute corruption cases. One could argue that journalists, watchdog groups and rank-and-file citizens with far fewer resources than the Illinois attorney general's office have done more to expose public corruption in the 15 years since she was elected.

It was the primary reason we couldn't endorse Madigan for re-election as attorney general in 2014. Questionable state greens, an unchecked anti-violence initiative under former Gov. Pat Quinn, patronage scandals, quid pro quos at Metra, double-dipping public-sector workers, Chicago's red light camera scandal, conflicts of interest, illegal campaign spending — we could go on — investigations of all these instances of public corruption unfurled in grand fashion, largely due to courageous voices outside the attorney general's office.

Twenty-eight House Republicans sent Madigan a letter Wednesday, calling on her office to investigate an ally of her father's, Illinois Auditor General Frank Mautino, whose campaign spending is under federal investigation. On a state election matter like this, where is she?

Well, Madigan recently joined other attorneys general calling for a special prosecutor in the case of President Donald Trump and his ties to Russia. Fair enough.

Yet she has looked the other way on countless scandals here at home.

To be clear, Madigan is not a lackluster elected official. She performs well in her chosen, yet narrow, terrain. We have praised her for her accomplishments in environmental advocacy, child protection and the toughening of penalties for sex offenders.

But she is compromised. She is incomplete. She cannot maximize the role of attorney general, as others have across the country, because she, her family, her supporters and her brand are interwoven with the fabric of clout that envelops this state. There is no way, or no willingness on her part, to pluck apart the fibers.

So the people of Illinois are left with an attorney general's office known mostly as a consumer protection bureau. That's part of the job for the attorney general of any state. But we're talking about the attorney general of a state notorious for public corruption, who won office assuring voters that she'd take "an active, hands-on role in cleaning up government. That's what people expect of their leaders and elected officials. And I will not let them down."

Madigan says she intends to run again for attorney general. Betting types would be wise to pledge their mortgages that she'll win.

Betting types could also wager, based on her record, that when corruption swirls and bangs into the public domain, it will be exposed, pursued and prosecuted by someone else.

I chose to include the article in this chapter about unions and the law because when she sent me the Whistleblower Information Intake Form, she asked what laws were being violated. At that time, I only knew that *Vaca v. Sipes* and *Hines v. Anchor Motor Freight* were the controlling federal laws regarding the duty of unions to represent their members.

The *Tribune* pulled no punches in pointing out the Illinois culture of sleaze, which included contract steering, bribery, patronage, obstruction, lying, and moneygrubbing. I chuckled when no mention of unions was made. But it was just two short years later when the newspaper reported that "Unions have too firm of a grip on Illinois government," and asked,

"Who is running Illinois government It's not the administration, It's not the department heads. It's the public employee unions."

The *Tribune* reported something that I wholeheartedly agreed with about Lisa Madigan's tenure as the state's chief legal officer. She spent too much time on consumer advocacy and not enough time on corruption busting. Interestingly, Madigan defended herself when she told the *Tribune* that she had statutory limitations when it came to prosecuting corruption. I recalled the time I saw her on television when she said, "My hands are tied." Throngs of people could be found who would testify that Lisa's father, long-serving Michael Madigan, helped pass the legislation that kept his daughter free from exposing movements union leaders continuously made to enrich themselves. In my response to Lisa Madigan's Whistleblower Information Intake Form, I informed her about FBI Agent Steve O'Reilly telling me that Illinois was not in accordance with laws about fair representation and labor unions. Nor was it abiding by the supremacy doctrine afforded by the Supreme Court. After receiving my report, she should have, it seemed to me, at least set forth an investigation to find out if unions were acting illegally.

The *Tribune* did not endorse Mrs. Madigan and stated that she assured voters she, "Would take an active, hands on role in cleaning up government. I will not let them down." However, the *Tribune*, in this article, stated that her office had become mostly a consumer protection bureau.

In my view, if the *Tribune* decided that the state could be better served by electing a new attorney general, this would have been a good time to use any material the paper had to show the public the tremendous influence unions have in Illinois government. I had supplied the paper with plenty of evidence, but even to this day, it flounders in the files of journalists.

CHAPTER 9

The Last Straw

Something had to cause me to cease and desist in my nearly three decades of finding justice for union members and exposing how unions took control of Illinois government. I nearly gave up when the IELRB and the Illinois Appellate Court rebuked US Supreme Court decisions regarding fair representation. I thought about giving up when *Chicago Tribune* reporter Jason Grotto first told me the story could be a series and then dropped it. When the FBI and the US attorney in Chicago decided not to investigate the unions almost made me fold the tent. I nearly gave up after I testified before a House Labor Committee in Springfield, and my state representative had his bill tabled because the unions lobbied against it. That bill would have brought Illinois's fair representation laws in line with controlling federal law. It was plenty discouraging when I learned the IELRB caters to unions and that unions had the power to craft their own laws. When my local state senator, Pam Althoff, told me, "This case is too old. Nothing can be done," and State Representative Jack Franks told me, "File your own lawsuit, and when you become a pauper, the state can help you," I became really discouraged. When I discovered legal defense organizations provided Mark Janus with financial and legal support while I was denied such support, I thought about giving up the fight.

Early on, I even thought it would not be worth my time to pursue how the IFT was ripping off members whose rights had been infringed. It was depressing when the IFT told me they didn't have the money to file a lawsuit for me and then gave Lisa Madigan and other politicians tons of money so they could get reelected.

All these reasons I overcame and continued to pursue justice. But when I learned about some of the following, I decided it was the last straw. One happenstance was an article that appeared in my local newspaper titled, "Another Legislative Ethics Placebo for the People of Illinois." It was lifted from the *Effingham Daily News*. The article stated, "The Illinois General Assembly is a master of approving phony reform bills." In addition, the paper reported that "Most bills are empty shells devoid of substantive, positive changes." What really told me it was time to stop fighting a fight that seemed impossible to win was when the article stated, "Obviously, lawmakers of this scandal-ridden state have shown they want nothing to do with changes that would undermine their ability to profit one way or another from their legislative duties." Continuing in the article, it revealed that "Super majority Democrats employed a familiar magic trick-creating an illusion of reform rather than real reform."

Legislative Inspector General Carol Pope was so disgusted by bills that did not pass, ones that could strengthen the authority of her office, that she resigned. The article stated, "It's a heck of a way to run a state. But this is, after all, business as usual in Illinois." The article was a big blow that helped me decide that, as the saying goes, enough is enough.

Although the article about sham bills and the state legislature giving illusions of reforming itself was a big blow that helped to end my crusade against the unions and the sleazy Illinois government, other things happened to end my quest to help aggrieved union members and expose the crooked unions and the runaway government.

In looking back on what happened to me in the fight against unions, I realized I wasn't in the right place at the right time. By that I mean I didn't learn about organizations that provided financial and legal help that could have helped me until it was too late. It was in the Janus article that I first learned about the National Right to Work Legal Defense Foundation. You can see by the email I received from Joe Rossell (photo 24) that the organization would have most likely filed a lawsuit for me after the IFT in Chicago refused me the US Supreme Court–mandated fair representation.

I corresponded with Mr. Rossell a couple times and asked him to file charges just as his foundation did in the Janus case. I was disappointed when I ran into a snag that prevented it from happening here in Illinois. The Right to Work Foundation claims its mission is, "to eliminate coercive union power and compulsory unionism." However, I asked Mr. Rossell to explain how or why his organization could not honor their mission and file charges aimed at coercive unionism in Illinois.

Mr. Rossell explained in his email that only workers can pursue legal action against unions that do not represent them. The foundation cannot unilaterally take legal action because any such action would have to come from a worker.

Dear Dr. Jones,

Thank you for your ongoing interest in the mission and efforts of the National Right to Work Foundation. I wanted to follow up to address your question regarding the need to refer workers to the Foundation.

The issue faced by the Foundation's legal team is that only workers with appropriate standing can pursue legal action against union bosses. Moreover, individual workers must agree to be represented by Foundation attorneys. (Unlike union bosses, we would never want to impose unwanted "representation" on workers.) As you probably know, third parties like the Foundation cannot simply pursue legal action against public unions unilaterally.

The perfect example of why the Foundation needs workers to ask for our assistance is the *Janus* case itself. As you may recall, former Illinois Governor Bruce Rauner first sued public sector unions to halt the seizure of forced dues and fees from public employees in Illinois arguing that after the Supreme Court's ruling in the 2014 *Harris v. Quinn* Foundation victory, such mandatory union payments clearly violated the First Amendment.

But a federal judge threw out Gov. Rauner's lawsuit because he did not have legal standing, since he would have needed to be a government worker who had been directly victimized by union bosses to pursue such a lawsuit. Even the governor lacked standing to challenge the forced union dues scheme because he was not personally having union dues seized from him.

It was only because a government employee like Mark Janus sought out Foundation legal assistance that the case was able to go forward. Ultimately Janus became the named plaintiff in the case against AFSCME when the governor was dismissed from the case, which is why the U.S. Supreme Court was eventually able to hear the case.

That is why we had suggested referring specific workers to seek Foundation legal assistance in order to challenge union corruption in Illinois. Foundation attorneys can only pursue legal action with the direct involvement and cooperation of individual workers who have been personally harmed by union officials.

If you know of specific workers who would benefit from Foundation legal assistance, please have them request free legal aid through the request form on the National Right to Work website (https://www.nrtw.org/free-legal-aid/) or by calling 1-800-336-3600.

Again, thank you for your ongoing interest in Right to Work.

In terms of what else could be done to combat union corruption in Illinois, I also wanted to offer one additional suggestion: While they are not as focused on legal action as the Foundation is, the Illinois Policy Institute (https://www.illinoispolicy.org/) has extensive media contacts in Illinois and may be able to help spotlight union corruption. So you might consider contacting them as well.

Thank you again.

Sincerely,

Joseph Rossell
National Right to Work Foundation

I was disappointed because it looked as though the foundation could have helped because a federal judge ruled that my case was meritorious. Hopefully, union workers will read this book, and if their rights have been infringed and their union didn't back them, then the Right to Work Foundation might be able to help them. It seems to me Mr. Rossell's organization could benefit by becoming better known to union members throughout the country. He was very accommodating and urged me to refer workers to his organization if they believed their unions were not representing them within the law. I'm sure there are many such cases going on in Illinois all the time, and union members could be helped more often than is currently being done.

Incidentally, the National Right to Work Legal Defense Foundation did file another suit on behalf of teachers who were members of the Chicago Teaches Union (CTU). Joanne Troesch and Ifeoma Nkemdi sued the CTU and the Chicago Board of Education over a union boss-created escape period that blocks workers from exercising their right to terminate union dues deductions from their paychecks outside the month of August. The teachers were supported with both financial and legal assistance.

Recall that in the Janus case, I had conversations with Mailee Smith, who did legal work with the Liberty Justice Center in Chicago. She also told me that "Fair representation cases are outside our expertise." It is still confusing to me why the Liberty Justice Center couldn't act against the unions that a good labor lawyer told me about. That action would be in violation of rights and deprivation of rights under color of law. Such legal action with the status of the Liberty Justice Center could help clean up union power in Illinois.

When Michael Madigan was indicted on twenty-two counts of public corruption, an interesting comment was made in an editorial in the *Chicago Tribune*. The comment was made by Governor J. B. Pritzker, who said, "This should be a wake-up call to everybody in public service that you better toe the line, you better do the right thing. You better stand up for the people that you represent and not try to line your own pockets." The *Tribune* said about the governor's comment, "Please, spare us, we've seen this movie before." Of course, that meant the paper believed that the governor was only providing the usual lip service and that nothing would be done to prevent agencies like the IELRB, the Illinois Appellate Court, and the Office of the Executive Inspector General to continue to protect the power unions had built up. The unions were heavy endorsers of Governor Pritzker during his campaign against Bruce Rauner.

The Illinois Policy Institute has a section called The Policy Shop. In it, the vice president of marketing, Austin Berg stated, "Madigan's gone, but the ethics problems remain. Even though Madigan has fallen, the corrupt system he put into place continues to hurt Illinois everyday ... and it must be dismantled. Real justice requires change beyond punishing the actions of one politician. It's time to fix the corrupt, failed institutions that fueled Madigan's unprecedented accumulation of power." Amen!

All the above added to my idea that I had done enough. And since I wasn't getting much help, I would just be spinning my wheels if I continued.

Incidentally, the Illinois Policy Institute published figures that showed big population drops in 2021. It is likely many people left the state because of the corruption going on. I knew about this from other sources, and it just added to my idea that this was the last straw.

Photos 25 and 26 are some political cartoons published in the *Chicago Tribune.*

IF WERE HONEST ABOUT OUR NEW LICENSE PLATE...

The cartoons also told me my battle against Illinois corruption wasn't going anywhere soon, and at age eighty-five, I had better things to do. Just look over the cartoons. What other state would go to such lengths to make fun of its chief legal officer and a speaker of the house? Ridiculous! Pitiful!

I really had not decided to write this book until I saw the cartoons. I consider them to be at least an influential part of my decision to admit defeat to the unions and the corrupt government. Actually, before totally giving up, I remembered an event in my life that took place in my hometown of Marion, Indiana. A wise, elderly businessman I happened to be talking to in my senior year of high school gave me some good advice. In a long conversation in his office, he told me, "Do the best you can with whatever you have, wherever you are."

I adopted this motto, and it has helped me to get through some tough times in my long life. I thought that to do the best I could after deciding not to contact people, I would have to do two things. One would be to write to President Joe Biden and tell him about how unions had taken over Illinois government. I would ask him to report to the Department of Justice and request some help from the federal government to make Illinois a more functional, democratic state, where honest elected officials ran the government, not coercive union bosses. His reply is shown in photo 27.

The very last thing I would do was to write a book and present the evidence I had accumulated about unions and government in a condensed, easy-to-understand way so there would be no doubt that the untold story about unions was now told.

THE WHITE HOUSE
WASHINGTON

November 5, 2021

Dr. Norman Harry Jones
Crystal Lake, Illinois

Dear Dr. Jones,

Thank you for taking the time to share your thoughts with me. Hearing from passionate individuals like you inspires me every day, and I welcome the opportunity to respond to your letter.

Our country faces many challenges, and the road we will travel together will be one of the most difficult in our history. Despite these tough times, I have never been more optimistic for the future of America. I believe we are better positioned than any country in the world to lead in the 21st century not just by the example of our power but by the power of our example.

While we may not always agree on how to solve every issue, I pledge to be a President for all Americans. I am confident that we can work together to find common ground to make America a more just, prosperous, and secure Nation.

As we move forward to address the complex issues of our time, I encourage you to remain an active participant in helping write the next great chapter of the American story. We need your courage and dedication at this critical time, and we must meet this moment together as the United States of America. If we do that, I believe that our best days still lie ahead.

Sincerely,

[signature]

I was disappointed with President Biden's reply because he took no interest in the problem I reported to him. I understood that unions were a big part of getting Joe Biden elected. Please read his letter, and you will see all he did was dance around the problems I told him Illinois was having. After reading his letter, I remember thinking that he did not address the problem I sent him. They addressed coercive union power and sleazy government officials.

In my state, as far as I was concerned, his words were the usual lip service politicians are good at. He, like many of the politicians in Illinois, helped to keep union tyranny a secret. If anybody should know that secrecy is the enemy of democracy, it is the President of the United States.

Now that you have read the letter from President Biden and you are reading the book, consider this the last straw in my attempt to tell the untold story about Illinois corruption.

CHAPTER 10

Conclusion and Recommendations

It is beyond my comprehension that any fair-minded person who has read the evidence presented herein and understands that an FBI spokesman told me, "This case belongs in federal court," would not believe the untold story about union corruption should land in federal court under the federal statute called the conspiracy against rights. To disagree with the evidence, much of which has to be prima facie, that I have compiled about union behavior coupled with government malfeasance would be alarming. Any lawyer who gives the evidence an honest review and doesn't accept it should go back to law school.

It was explained to me by an experienced labor lawyer that there is another federal statute being violated in Illinois. It is known as the deprivation of rights under color of law.

Any conclusion about a case that some are trying to hide is difficult to prove and then make public. As stated in chapter 1, I believe unions started their scheme to accumulate money so they could do two things important to them: pay union employees high salaries and have enough money to fight legal battles that come their way that, if lost as in the Janus case, could hurt progress.

It is more than likely that the Terry Knapp case in 1983 in Peoria is where the unions' plot to enrich themselves started. Two US Supreme Court decisions in the 1960s held that unions are compelled to use union dues to protect the civil rights of members. Terry Knapp won his First Amendment case against the Peoria school board, which went all the way to the Supreme Court. However, Mr. Knapp noted that after the courts awarded him about $350,000, "The union lawyers took most of it." That should not have happened; Knapp deserved to keep the money in accordance with federal statutes. By taking money from Knapp's earnings, the unions began their campaign to cheat union members so they could keep their coffers healthy. The IFT-AFT represented Knapp, and as this is written, that union persists in not filing meritorious lawsuits to protect its members. This act is part of my conclusion that there is a gigantic conspiracy raging in Illinois that involves unions attempt to stay solvent.

Several things happened that gave away the union plot to accumulate enough money to pay union employees high salaries and contribute to campaign funds of politicians who do favors for unions. It wasn't a miracle that the IEA, CTU, and the UAW joined the plot to save unions money. A clue was given by Tonya Exum, when she courageously submitted an op-ed to the *Chicago Tribune* that revealed her union, the UAW, was not protecting her from sexual harassment.

The Illinois Policy Institute concluded that "Illinois goes to great lengths to cater to union officials." Another clue that helped me conclude that a conspiracy against rights was silently taking place was when some pregnant teachers in the CTU had to call in the US Department of Justice to stop a principal from harassing teachers to get back to work despite leave for pregnancy. Why didn't the CTU support the harassed teachers? What are unions for?

It helped reveal part of the union's plot when the Illinois Policy Institute published charts about how unions spent their money. Exactly how much was being spent for representation was not clearly spelled out. No mention was made about the amount spent by individual unions on lawsuits. Probably because there weren't any!

The federal statute regarding the conspiracy against rights should be easy for most people to understand, but the deprivation of rights under color of law needs clarification. It is a federal criminal charge that is sometimes used against the police and other law enforcement officers when they allegedly use their power to violate a person's rights under the US Constitution or laws of the United States. Or said in a slightly different way, it makes it a crime to use power given to a government agency to deprive or conspire willfully to deprive a person of any right protected by the Constitution or laws of the United States. It is a serious crime punishable by prison terms or fines. As I was introduced to those statutes, I wondered if those in law enforcement in Illinois could be charged. It seemed to me the judges on the Illinois Appellate Court who ruled that "Unions have no obligation to back their members," could be guilty of using their power to cater to unions. Same goes for members of the IELRB, who admitted to "crafting" their own laws. And it looked like the evidence exposed herein about unions makes state agencies like the IELRB, the Illinois inspector general, and the attorney general very suspect of being guilty under the deprivation of rights under color of law statute. I'm also wondering if the entire Illinois Educational Labor Relations Act is illegal. It does state entries that seem to modify and change US Supreme Court decisions. As previously mentioned, to include in the act that union members seeking legal help and union financing must prove "intentional misconduct" on the part of the union in order to prove an unfair labor practice seems aimed at depriving union members of their right to be protected.

It could certainly be concluded that when I was told by Ralph Locke of the IELRB that "We cater to unions. You'll see," it should have warranted an investigation. Wasn't it a probable deprivation of rights when in a letter from IELRB board member Keith Snyder he admitted, "Unions had virtually a free hand to write the laws they prefer"? And wasn't it close to depriving people of their rights when Janet Doyle of the Office of the Inspector General stated that regarding labor laws, state laws take precedence over federal laws? Remember the case I presented in the chapter about unions and the law that stated fair representation cases are governed solely by federal law? I now wonder how close Illinois state senator Pam Althoff came to depriving union members of their rights when she told me, "This case is too old. Nothing can be done." And I wonder if state lawmakers came close to depriving union members of their rights when none took action when I sent out 114 emails asking for an investigation into union activities.

I question if Attorney General Lisa Madigan engaged in depriving union members of their rights when she ignored the contents of the Whistleblower Information Intake Form she sent me, and which I filed with her office. In the form, she asked for specific laws being violated. And I gave them. I was not given a reason why the laws I gave didn't apply. I wondered then if she intentionally dismissed my case because to launch an investigation could hurt unions in their effort to build funds—and contribute to her campaign coffer.

I concluded that when Lisa Madigan stated on TV that her hands were tied when it came to investigating corruption, an investigation should have been launched to find out just what tied the hands of the chief legal officer in the state. Doesn't the public have the right to know what is going on in state government that prevents the attorney general from investigating corruption? Walter Cronkite might turn over in his grave since it was he who said, "One of the main duties of the press is to monitor the performance of government."

When I asked for help, why didn't someone in authority check out the tainted summaries of fair representation cases issued by the IELRB and published in the *Public Employee Review*? For authorities in Illinois to allow this practice of avoiding the truth is preposterous and should be stopped immediately. Is omitting facts a crime?

In my attempts to expose the obvious conspiracy involving unions and government, the FBI told me media exposure of such crimes might move the case up the FBI's priority list. I found out just how difficult it can be to obtain that exposure. And I still wonder why the onus is on citizens filing complaints to get that exposure. The case I am still trying to expose is still, it seems, not very high on the FBI priority list. A case this important and holds huge implications for an honest state government should not be so easily brushed aside. The *Chicago Tribune* did have a chance to expose the case when it stated, "Who is running state government? It's not the administration. It's not the department heads. It's the public employee unions." Sadly, the newspaper missed its chance to contribute to exposing the crooked unions and shady politicians when it failed to publish any follow-up articles.

In the Janus case, in which the US Supreme Court ruled that nonunion members could not have dues taken from their paychecks, it was alarming that staunch union leaders began filing bills that would weaken the ruling. This would have been a good time to publicize the names of politicians who benefited from union money. Once they were identified, they could be watched to see if any moves they made were attempts to deprive union members of their rights. Plus, citizens would have a better idea of who to vote for.

There must somehow be penalties assessed when citizens file complaints with their representatives in government, and those representatives do not respond. Such a rule would at least make government more responsible. I wrote to Senator Dick Durbin and State Senator Melinda Bush and never heard from them. It is of little wonder that Illinois is said to be the most corrupt state in America.

I continued to determine that Illinois government is crooked when I did hear from Illinois state representative Martin McLaughlin. He said something very profound: "I do believe that public labor unions influence on Democratic legislation is one of the great obstacles to overcome." I figured he might be the one courageous lawmaker to talk to the federal government and find out if democratic legislation is always legit. I never heard from him. It seemed to me that in my years of trying to expose Illinois government and the unions that control them, many lawmakers knew that their colleagues tried to pass illegal bills that helped unions obtain their power but did nothing about it.

As I wrote this book after two decades of trying to expose the cowardly unions and misguided government officials, I thought it might be helpful to make conclusions and recommendations about the tyranny. Such conclusions and recommendations might inspire some courageous politicians or legal authorities to launch an investigation and stop the union insurrection.

Let me try something here. I am going to give you examples of conversations I had with two people who worked in a law enforcement agency. They were McHenry County state attorney Patrick Kenneally (see a letter from him on page 58), and FBI Agent Steve O'Reilly. Once you read here what each had to say, decide what would be your conclusion. Then I will give you mine.

First, recall the many conversations I had with Agent O'Reilly. After

I sent him my plethora of evidence, he told me, "This case belongs in federal court." I asked what the grounds for the suit would be, and he said, "Illinois is not abiding by the supremacy doctrine afforded the United States Supreme Court." By that he meant that the state was not adhering to controlling federal laws regarding unions providing fair representation to their members. He made it clear to me that state agencies—like the General Assembly, the IELRB, and the Illinois Appellate Court—were modifying federal laws in order to cater to union whims. Agent O'Reilly clarified for me that the way unions and state agencies were currently operating was "under the radar" and should be investigated.

Years after my contact with Agent O'Reilly, I contacted my local state's attorney, Patrick Kenneally, and essentially told him what Agent O'Reilly told me. In fact, I sent Mr. Kenneally my full packet of evidence and asked what could be done to get the unions and their cohorts into court. In his answer to me, he wrote, "The short answer is that very little is being done to counteract the influence of unions on Illinois. Rather, just the opposite. Unions are being supported, financed and encouraged by State officials." He went on to say, "As you may know, unions are protected under both federal and state laws." He further stated, "While in my opinion, much of their activity is counterproductive and causes more problems than it fixes, nothing they are doing is illegal, per se. As such, there is very little I or any other official who is not in the legislature can do to address many of the concerns that you and I have."

My conclusion was that something was drastically wrong when the federal government tells a citizen filing a complaint about union corruption that the case belongs in federal court, and the state government tells that same citizen that in regard to union corruption, nothing they are doing is illegal.

RECOMMENDATIONS

As anyone might guess, my first recommendation is to find a solution to unions refusing to file lawsuits to protect the civil rights of members. As Agent O'Reilly pointed out, they must adhere to US Supreme Court decisions, and they are not doing that. And they are probably not doing that to save money. My recommendation is to have union leadership find a solution before they are forced to do so. If they don't, then it is likely that many union leaders could find themselves in prison for conspiring to alter the rights of their members. I would think it should be legal for union leaders and members to agree that union lawyers retain 20 percent of whatever amount union members received from a verdict or settlement from an unscrupulous employer. For example, in the Knapp case, the IFT-AFT lawyers would have been paid 20 percent of the $350,000 Knapp was awarded, or $70,000. I know the federal laws that I have mentioned state that unions are responsible to use their funds to back a member and are not allowed to, as in the Knapp case, recover any money from a winning verdict for a dues-paying member. However, if both the union members and the union leaders agree, there would likely not be a need to adhere to the federal statute.

I urge media outlets to be more aggressive in reporting on questionable union activity. The Tonya Exum op-ed is a good example of the *Chicago Tribune* trying to expose how unions cheat their members by not backing them, allowing the unions to keep money in their coffers. Why my op-eds were never published is a good example of a newspaper playing favorites and limiting union exposure. In my opinion, the *Chicago Tribune* is partially responsible for perpetuating union power by not digging deeper into illegal actions of unions.

A change in the policies of unions would benefit Illinois. For example, the IEA-NEA could take down a phrase on its website and follow the law when it states that "If you need legal help you can get that help at rates below usual attorney fees." This admits this union tries to circumvent the standing law as it is telling members they will have to pay for lawsuits.

The IELRB, the office of the Illinois inspector general, the courts, and the Illinois attorney general should turn over new leaves and stop unions from cheating members when it comes to using union money to defend member rights. This union plot to save money, backed by politicians and many in law enforcement, must be investigated by the federal government in Chicago. If that isn't done, then union influence, union power, and union money will maintain a firm grip on Illinois government.

Some law enforcement agency must look into union finances. I mentioned before that the Illinois Policy Institute published a well-done report on union finances. However, I noted that it needs to be found out exactly what the word "representation" means. I urge an investigation, probably by the federal government, to find out how much unions spent on lawsuits the last several years. I think the results would be surprising. And when it is discovered that few if any lawsuits were filed, legal action should be taken to correct this situation.

Indictments should be issued against those who cater to unions. The contents within this book should give any law enforcement agency a good start on who these people are. I'm hoping for massive arrests to be made as this would give fair warning to people running for office or in offices that they better stay clear of any catering to unions.

The Illinois General Assembly should form a committee to see to it that US Supreme Court decisions are quickly adopted in Illinois. Illinois probably disregards these decisions more than any other state. Laws enacted by the Supreme Court are the laws of the land, and the land of Lincoln should upgrade its policies and attitudes about adopting them.

There is no question that the IELRB, the Illinois Appellate Court, and other law enforcement agencies should be fully investigated by the federal government. The flimsy excuses the feds give for allowing unions to take control of government is a major problem in this combine state. It is ridiculous for an FBI agent to tell me years ago that a case belongs in federal court, and yet no case has been filed to this day.

To let the unions have the power to insert their own language, like "intentional misconduct," and to have the privilege to craft their own laws, as they admitted to, and to modify federal statutes is pathetic government. The IELRB should no longer be allowed to publish tainted reviews in the *Public Employee Review*, but such behavior continues and will continue until the FBI or the US attorney steps up.

One thing I know that would help to stop corruption is to enact a law that punishes lawmakers when it can be shown that it was reported to them a law was being broken, and they did nothing to stop it. For example, a union member might report that his or her union was intentionally circumventing using its funds and lawyers to support a member whose rights were infringed by an employer. If the lawmaker doesn't act, and it can be shown in some form of documentation that he or she didn't, then a fine or prison time would put a big dent in Illinois corruption. An example of this is when I mentioned that I contacted my local state senator, Pam Althoff, and told her how the unions were, in essence, stealing money from their members. She responded that "This case is too old. Nothing can be done." The documentation involving her would be her email to me that told me she was ignoring my plea. As things stand now, laws to stop such inaction in Illinois will not happen because the very people who would have to enact such a law are the ones who would suffer from its adoption.

Judges in Illinois should be more intently scrutinized. For example, I showed where Illinois Appellate Court judges rebuked federal law when some of them ruled, "Unions have no obligation to fund law suits for members." To this day, I don't know why this documented piece of evidence has not led to indictments of the judges who helped make it. Years ago, Illinois judges went to prison because they were found to fix cases. This case was known as the Greylord case, and I think we have similar actions by current judges on the Illinois Appellate Court. At the very least, when the current Illinois Appellate Court held that "Unions have no obligation" to fund lawsuits for members, it should have been quickly investigated by the FBI. The FBI inaction is killing Illinois as unions illegally accumulate money by not spending dues revenue to protect members' rights. And, of course, that money goes to those perpetuating union power. It is pitiful that Illinois judges go unchecked and, therefore, contribute to union corruption in Illinois.

Now that Michael Madigan is no longer pulling the strings in the General Assembly, lawmakers should be more honest and make certain that a bill is not tabled when it is intended to bring Illinois law in line with US Supreme Court decisions. When committee members meet to hear testimony from citizens, they should not be allowed to talk on their cell phones, read newspapers, and talk in whispers in small groups like kindergartners.

No state should require its citizens to exact a price simply because the attorney general in that state has his or her hands tied when it comes to investigating corruption. As shown in this book, Illinois attorney general Lisa Madigan admitted her hands were tied when it came to investigating corruption. Only someone living in a cave would believe that her father wasn't responsible for enacting a law in Illinois that actually gave corrupt individuals the right to do as they pleased. Recall that I spent hours filling out the Whistleblower Information Intake Form Lisa Madigan sent me unsolicited, only to have her ignore the evidence I had and the FBI confirmed. From now on, attorneys general in Illinois should be governed by a watchdog of some kind so whistleblowers have a chance to be heard.

It is not against the law for politicians to accept donations from unions, but it might be worth considering that donations should not be accepted for those who work in law enforcement agencies. Just a thought, but there is no doubt that money influences union control of Illinois government. The Madigans received millions from big unions.

Another law I recommend be enacted would be one about members of law enforcement agencies wantonly and intentionally ignore controlling federal laws. I refer to when I mentioned that I reported to the executive inspector general that unions were cheating members. I received an answer from Janet Doyle, an assistant in that office. In a terrifying response, she told me that in matters of labor law, state law takes precedence over federal law. Here is another example of someone in law enforcement misrepresenting the truth to further the agenda of unions. Such dishonesty should bring punishment, like fines or imprisonment. Ms. Doyle pointed out that her office, "was created to investigate misconduct in the agencies, boards and commissions responsible to the Governor." It seems in this case that the law was in place but intentionally avoided. This is where my recommendation comes in, whereby those ignoring the law should be punished.

"Fraudulent concealment" is a legal term that should come into play far more often in Illinois than it currently does. Politicians and others wanting to ignore things that would affect their contributions from shady unions are experts at purposefully omitting the facts in matters that affect their standings.

Illinois and all other states should strengthen their abilities to abide by the supremacy doctrine afforded by the US Supreme Court. Agent O'Reilly made a very strong point with me when he told me about how Illinois was not adhering to that law. Not doing so helps unions maintain their firm grips on Illinois government.

Complaints citizens make to the media in Illinois don't always get the proper exposure. Editor Kristen McQueary of the *Chicago Tribune* seemed to realize that as she said, "Citizens complaints should not be universally brushed aside." Although newspapers have freedom of the press, they all, especially in corrupt Illinois, should regard it as their duty to monitor government. This cannot be law but a necessity in fighting crime.

In my view, there are not nearly enough organizations like the National Right to Work Legal Defense Foundation and the Liberty Justice Center in existence to protect worker rights. Workers often don't have the money to file charges against employers, and when their unions abandoned them, it often caused tremendous problems. I have often felt that many workplace shootings were caused by unions neglecting to take quick action against unscrupulous employers. It might be a good idea for Congress to upgrade the conspiracy against rights statute as stronger enforcement of this could curtail violence.

In my final recommendation, I told you I would discuss in further detail correspondence I had with Agent Steve O'Reilly and the state's attorney for McHenry County, Patrick Kenneally. Remember that Agent O'Reilly told me, "This case belongs in federal court," and he mentioned that, "Illinois is not abiding by the supremacy doctrine afforded the US Supreme Court." He made it clear that Illinois agencies were manipulating federal law and generally dancing around federal statutes. On the other hand, State's Attorney Kenneally, in a shocking comment about unions said, "Nothing they are doing is illegal, per se." I think Mr. Kenneally is honest, but then again, there are those in positions like his in Illinois who do all they can to side with unions. Isn't it easy to see by these two law enforcement officials, making almost opposite statements, that there is no cohesion, no agreement, no coordination between the federal government and the Illinois state government? This is obviously a prodigious problem. So I have to recommend that the feds and Illinois officials work hard to bring better government to all citizens of Illinois. It is ridiculous to have such a gap in the two governments. I propose periodic meetings to discuss anything that resembles corruption.

An example of what the lack of government agreement can do is that I received letters from both the FBI and the office of the US district attorney in 2007, proving they knew about unions and state government wrecking Illinois government. But as this is written in 2022, unions are still on a rampage to control Illinois government, and nothing is being done. That is not democracy. It is tyranny.

In ending this book, I'm reminded of what legendary journalist Edward R. Murrow once said: "The obscure we see eventually, the completely apparent takes longer."

ABOUT THE AUTHOR

 For four decades, Dr. Norman Jones has published books and made presentations about leadership, communications, teaching, and human development. He is now retired. He graduated from high school in Marion, Indiana, in 1954 and was awarded the Kiwanis Achievement Award for basketball. He earned a varsity letter for basketball at Manchester College and two letters at Ball State University. He earned a BA degree in education in 1959 and a MA degree in counseling and guidance in 1963 from Ball State. Dr. Jones became a head coach in basketball, baseball, and golf while teaching at high schools in North Vernon and Salem, Indiana, and in Palatine, Illinois.

In 1977, he was granted a sabbatical from the Palatine school district and earned a doctorate in counseling and educational psychology from the University of Mississippi. In 1981, Dr. Jones published *Keep in Touch* with Prentice-Hall. He then founded Communication Unlimited and began his writing and speaking career. He appeared on WBBM-TV (CBS) in Chicago on the talk show *Common Ground* and was on WIND and WBBM radio shows.

Dr. Jones published *Performance Management in the 21ˢᵗ Century* with St. Lucie/CRS Press. He taught graduate courses, including Human Development for Secondary School Administrators at Roosevelt University in Chicago, and Principles of Guidance at Northeastern Illinois University. He made presentations for Blue Cross-Blue Shield, the Illinois State Board of Education, the International Graphoanalysis Society, and the University of Wisconsin football staff. He published his memoir, *Growing Up in Indiana: The Culture & Hoosier Hysteria Revisited,* and then *Main St. vs. Wall Street: Wake-up Calls for America's Leaders* in 2010. He has published two articles for the Indiana Historical Society Press magazine *Traces.*

During his retirement, he has made an effort to help the state of Illinois lose its moniker of being the most corrupt state in America. Part of that effort is told in this book with the appropriate title, *The Untold Story about How Unions Took Over Illinois Government.*

> The obscure we see eventually, the completely apparent takes longer.
>
> —Edward R. Murrow

Made in the USA
Columbia, SC
01 October 2022

68370646R00067